LITERARY PEDAGOGICS
AFTER
DECONSTRUCTION

THE DOLPHIN

General Editor: Tim Caudery

22

LITERARY PEDAGOGICS AFTER DECONSTRUCTION

Scenarios and Perspectives
in the Teaching of English Literature

Edited by Per Serritslev Petersen

AARHUS UNIVERSITY PRESS

Word-processed at the Department of English, Aarhus University
Printed in Denmark by Special-trykkeriet, Viborg
Published with financial support from the University Research Foundation

General Editor: Tim Caudery

Editorial address:
The Dolphin
Department of English, Aarhus University
DK-8000 Aarhus C

Distribution:
Aarhus University Press
Building 170, Aarhus University
DK-8000 Aarhus C
Fax: +45 86 19 84 33

ISBN 87 7288 372 3
ISSN 0106-4487
The Dolphin no. 22, Spring issue 1992

Subscription price for one year (two issues):
Europe 198 DKK, Overseas US$ 38.00.
Single copy price (not including postage):
Europe 118 DDK, overseas US$ 19.65.
Back issues available - list sent on request.

Contents

Front cover text: from the American poet John Ashbery's ironic critique of the intellectual mirror games of postmodern criticism in 'Self-Portrait in a Convex Mirror' (1975).

... *Today has no margins, the event arrives*
Flush with its edges, is of the same substance,
Indistinguishable. "Play" is something else;
It exists, in a society specifically
Organized as a demonstration of itself.
There is no other way, and those assholes
Who would confuse everything with their mirror games
Which seem to multiply stakes and possibilities, or
At least confuse issues by means of an investing
Aura that would corrode the architecture
Of the whole in a haze of suppressed mockery,
Are beside the point. They are out of the game,
Which doesn't exist until they are out of it.
It seems like a very hostile universe
But as the principle of each individual thing is
Hostile to, exists at the expense of all others
As philosophers have often pointed out, at least
This thing, the mute, undivided present,
Has the justification of logic, which
In this instance isn't a bad thing
Or wouldn't be, if the way of telling
Didn't somehow intrude, twisting the end result
Into a caricature of itself....

(Lines 421-43)

Preface

Après la Déconstruction le déluge? Well, to judge from the varied contributions to this book, the current situation in the literary-studies classroom could perhaps be seen as a deluge of hermeneutical/pedagogical theories and strategies. But it is a deluge, not so much in the sense of unabashedly endorsing the postmodern ethos of 'total abandon' or 'anything goes', but, I hope, in the sense of offering the prospective reader a cornucopia of stimulating suggestions and discussions on how to teach English literature in these *fin-de-siècle* times. This hope, at least, formed an integral part of my editorial motivation and intention when I first conceived the idea of a *Dolphin* issue on literary pedagogics in the 1990s and launched the project at an international English Studies conference, the 1990 Sandbjerg Conference, organized by my own department under the thematic heading of 'present trends, future options', that is, the trends and options for English Studies in both a national and an international perspective. As Roger D. Sell points out in his contribution to this book, a joint project like this could, hopefully, provide a forum for an international debate on literary pedagogics which would 'make us more self-conscious about what we are doing, precisely because we shall start to compare and contrast the configuration of human and institutional variables in our own situation with those obtaining in other educational set-ups'.

When I started soliciting contributions from colleagues across the world, I sketched out a tentative agenda for the project. First, I simply asked contributors to 'discuss *their* idea of what constitutes a good literary seminar and, by way of illustration, outline a pedagogical scenario for such a seminar'. Second, I suggested that some of the following questions could be pondered upon:

What kind of objectives, educational and otherwise, did you have in mind when you decided to teach that particular seminar?

How did those objectives impinge upon the practical organization of the seminar, your choice of the pedagogical nuts and bolts (say, use of introductory lecture or synopsis, study groups, assignments, hand-outs etc.)?

How did you strike the pedagogical balance, if any, between a 'teacherly' or 'masterminding' containment of the progression of the seminar and the potential anarchy of active student participation in, say, setting up agendas for the class discussions?

The question of literary studies ('reading books') as a somewhat anachronistic academic exercise *vis-à-vis* media or cultural studies.

I would like, at this stage, to express my gratitude to the contributors for their generous interest in and commitment to the project which has now, at long last, materialized in book form. As far as the organization of the contents is concerned, I have chosen first to focus on discussions and scenarios relating primarily to the teaching of Shakespearean drama in Scandinavian universities (Roger D. Sell, Niels Bugge Hansen, Karl-Heinz Westarp). After the drama section, the focus is shifted to other genres, notably poetry, and the current pedagogical/educational issues involved in such teaching, theoretical as well as practical (Lars Ole Sauerberg, Marianne Thormählen). Then follows a section devoted to Women's Studies in the form of field reports and reflections on specific courses/seminars comprising feminist theory and practice (Suzette Henke, Dorrit Einersen and Ingeborg Nixon). In the following section, feminism is replaced by historicism, both in a Marxist and in a Popperian version, as the hermeneutical/pedagogical issue under debate (Christopher Hampton, Per Serritslev Petersen). The book concludes with a discussion – and textual illustration – of *rewriting* in literary studies, the pedagogical/educational objective being to 'return [the students'] critical and theoretical knowledge to the originating text by re-writing it' and thus, ideally, make them 'become active re-makers of their world, rather than cleverly passive outsiders' (Robert Clark).

So much for the 'cornucopia' I have to offer in this book. *Embarras de richesse*? Whatever, *bon appétit!*

Per Serritslev Petersen
May 1992

Teaching Shakespeare on Literary Pragmatic Principles

Roger D. Sell, Åbo Akademi University, Finland

1. Contexts of writing and reading/performance

Literary pragmatics is an approach to literature which very explicitly emphasizes the importance of contextualization. Pragmatics was originally, and still is, that branch of linguistic scholarship which, recognizing that the relationship between the signifier and the signified is purely arbitrary and conventional, studies the ways in which language utterances acquire particular meaning and interactive force through being used in particular situations within sociocultural contexts. The simplest illustration is that the utterance 'Could you open a window?' will vary in the effect it produces, depending on whether or not the person or persons hearing it 'understand' (as we put it) English, and on whether it is addressed by, say, a professor to a group of students in a stuffy seminar room or by a doctor to a patient under examination for a hand injury. Up until the mid-1980s most pragmatic analysis had been carried out on similar cases of spoken language use in contemporary social intercourse. Considerably less work was done on written use, and very little at all on literary activity. Sooner or later the expansion of interests was bound to occur, however, and in literary pragmatics the continuities with pragmatic research in general are still clear. The important thing to grasp is that literary pragmatics is not primarily concerned with linguistic interaction between the characters portrayed in literary texts, but between the real writers or speakers of literary texts and their real readers or listeners. Basically, the aim is to relate the production and reception of literary texts to all or some of the linguistic and sociocultural contexts in which those processes take place.

This inevitably involves interdisciplinarity. Whereas much of the present century's linguistic and literary scholarship has tended towards a fragmenting specialization which has separated the study of language from the study of literature, and both of them from the study of society at large, literary pragmatics draws on concepts and methods developed within twentieth-century literary, linguistic and historical research with the aim of bringing them together within a single frame of reference. The ambition may seem somewhat reminiscent of a much older philology.

It was only in the 1970s that linguistic research began to come closer, as one might say, to real human beings, and to contexts of language use. This tendency can now be traced in developments as different as speech-act theory, discourse analysis, conversation analysis, anthropological linguistics, psycholinguistics, sociolinguistics and, most centrally, pragmatics. Still more generally, there is now a growing interest among linguists in working on corpora of live language data. And since the 1980s, there has also been a very strong reaction against de-contextualizing approaches to literature. Within a Marxist perspective, there has been much discussion of how texts come to be designated as literary in the first place; this is to no small extent a matter of forces at work in society and culture at large (cf. Eagleton 1983:1-16). 'New' historians (e.g. Greenblatt 1980) have developed fascinating and unexpected aspects of the consubstantiality of literary texts with the cultures in which they are written and read, and even the more traditional historical approach to literature has renewed itself, not least by establishing closer links between the tasks of the bibliographer and those of the critic: the literary text's circumstances of publication have been brought into the very centre of the interpretative arena (cf. McGann 1985). Somewhat similarly, *Rezeptions-ästhetik* has relativised the significance of literary works to the horizons of expectations of particular audiences (cf. Jauss 1982), while German and Dutch empirical literary scientists have tested the responses of particular groups of real readers (cf. Schmidt 1982). At the same time, the West's discovery of Bakhtin (e.g. Bakhtin 1981) has led to insights into relationships between the languages of literature and the wide range of sociolects – the heteroglossia – operative within any language community. With contextualization so firmly established as a common denominator in both linguistic and literary thought by the mid-1980s, the development of literary pragmatics was inevitable.

Like pragmatic research in general, literary pragmatics has come to embrace a very wide range of enquiry (see Sell forthcoming (a)). On the one hand it reveals, as does Anglo-American linguistic pragmatics (e.g. Leech 1983), concerns which are still fairly close to the syntax and semantics of mainstream linguistics; the analysis often sticks narrowly to texts. On the other hand it reveals, as does the continental tradition of pragmatics (e.g. Verschueren 1987), concerns ranging towards anthropological linguistics, sociolinguistics, psycholinguistics and ideological critique; discussion sometimes embraces the broadest kind of context. There are also middle-of-the-road literary pragmaticists, who reflect both these types of concern and try to catch the dynamic relationship between a text and its various contexts of sending and reception most directly.

But how can one ever actually describe a context? There comes a point when literary pragmaticists wish to avoid the epistemological naivety of traditional biographers, historians and philologists and begin to echo the hermeneutic doubts of present-day literary theorists. Most radically of all, can we even be sure that there are, and always have been, a world and other people 'out there'? And even if we can, how much confidence can we have in our own knowledge of them? – such knowledge as we may have being intimately bound up with the language we use in order to describe things. Then again, a description reflects a particular viewpoint and, once made, can be interpreted by different people in different ways. Even historians nowadays present accounts that are relativistically decentered, treating verbal evidence as multivalent, and speaking less of absolute events than of particular narratives. All of which can only mean that what Helen Gardner (1959) called a writer's historical and human context is far more problematic than was once thought. And if we cannot be sure of contexts, the same must apply to what E.D. Hirsch (1967, 1973) called the author's meaning, which is supposed to be interpretable from them.

On the other hand, literary pragmaticists sometimes find that literary theory is rather distant from literary phenomena. This is where they may sound more like old-fashioned historical and philological scholars, but their reasoning has less to do with historical purism than with the pragmatism of William James or Richard Rorty. The point is that, for members of a community and cultural tradition, a writer's historical and human context, and an author's meaning, do become *virtually* real. People *think* they know some things, and they are prepared to work towards some general agreement as to what might be true. They behave *as if* certain things are true, and this imagined or negotiated 'truth' is what they assume and rely on all the time in their actions. They tacitly appeal to it as a context in which to place linguistic utterances, written or spoken, literary or non-literary, and without such habitual cross-reference to an assumed world, language would not function at all. Pragmatics is the study of the interrelationship between uses of language and the contexts of putative circumstances and assumed world-knowledge in which they become meaningful, effective and affective.

As readers of Shakespeare, then, we behave as if, thanks to our own efforts and the expert help of historians, philologians and others, we can know a sociocultural and linguistic context within which his texts were used for the first time, and which was more or less common to Shakespeare, his fellow actors and the Elizabethan and Jacobean audience. This putative context of the original community is the one I shall refer to as 'the Shakespearian context'. Our normal unspoken assumption is that Shakespeare tacitly relied on it to give his words meaning and interactive force for his contemporaries, and that his contemporaries, tacitly cross-referring to this same context, believed that they did indeed understand him. It may well be that we can never really know whether one person understands another; silent passivity is probably only one of many disguises that incomprehension can adopt, and incomprehension need not even be conscious. But in practice we usually assume that people have understood us until they say or do something sufficiently odd to suggest the contrary. By the same token we tend to assume that what Shakespeare meant was what his contemporaries understood, and that by an effort of historical imagination we can understand much the same things too.

Yet even this way of putting it, with all its hedgings and reservations, is still a simplification. Not only must countless aspects of any Shakespearian context now be quite beyond recall; for us who live in the late twentieth century, a thousand and one other things come crowding in upon us which could never have been present to Shakespeare. Suppose, for instance, that we have grown up in Britain and are familiar with what is loosely thought of as the English cultural tradition. Then we cannot turn our glance back and reconstruct the putative Shakespearian context without also thinking of Keats's remarks about negative capability, of Kean's Shylock or Garrick's Hamlet, of Johnson's remarks on 'peeps through the blanket of the dark', and so on. Even gossip about Shakespeare the man – Why did he leave his second best bed to his wife? Did he go poaching in his youth? – forms part of the tissue of associations with which he comes down to us (see Sell, forthcoming (b)). During the course of time, Shakespeare and Shakespearian texts have fed manifold kinds of interest and released many well-known responses and interpretations, all of which now form part of the world within which we interpret. As classics, indeed, the texts are even more profoundly communal than they were for the original audience; they have been the focus of a centuries-long tradition of discussion, and contain stories, characters and phrases which bind together all of us who carry them in our heads, so that aspects of life in our own day and age are for ever being drawn into the Shakespearian orbit. In early 1991 we may well find ourselves wondering: 'Is Saddam Hussein of Iraq more like Richard III or Macbeth?'

But what, then, is the position of a Swedish-Finland reader of Shakespeare? We might be tempted to diagram this as shown in Figure 1. Yet this would be a distortion. The British context of 1991 is not privileged by a uniquely unbroken and perpendicular descent from the Shakespearian context. Although non-British students of modern Britain and of the British interpretation of Shakespeare do at first direct their attention to both the current and earlier British contexts 'from the side', once they have done so they begin to integrate them as part of their own associative networks, so that in part they read like an Englishman. Furthermore, Shakespeare is often already an integral element in their own mother-tongue culture. For Swedish Finns, Shakespeare has been known through both German, Swedish and Finnish translations, and through local acting traditions.

My predecessor's predecessor as Professor of English Language and Literature at Åbo Akademi, the university of Swedish Finland, wrote, in Swedish, a monograph on Swedish translations of *Macbeth* (Donner 1950), and

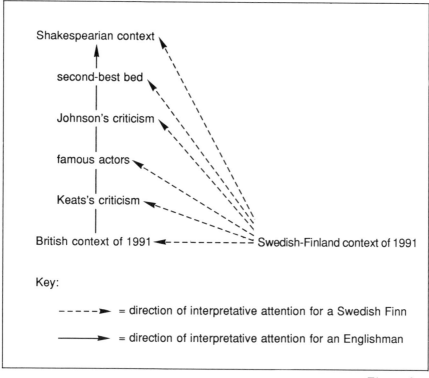

Figure 1.

my colleague, the present Professor of Comparative Literature, has produced a brilliant Finland-Swedish translation of *Hamlet* which makes the hero seem like a Nylanning. A more accurate model would therefore diagram Shakespeare as the centre of a circle of which many different cultural traditions form the radii, except that somehow one also ought to show that British people tend to be introspective in their Shakespeare tradition, whereas people in other cultures turn their attention in several different directions. Swedish Finns, in their awareness of both their own and other traditions, including the British, in effect belong to more than one community. For them, Shakespeare is potentially a far richer cultural experience than for an Englishman, just as an Englishman's experience of Dante, which includes Dante as mediated by the Pre-Raphaelites, has the same kind of advantage over an Italian's.

So texts are for ever being recontextualized. On the one hand, readers, scholars, directors, actors are for ever trying to re-live the Shakespearian context, and any university teacher of Shakespeare inevitably tries to set students on this path of recovery. On the other hand, an enormous pressure is

13

exerted by post-Shakespearian contexts, and especially by the sociocultural context of whatever happens to be the here and now. Indeed, in any given country's cultural tradition, the resistance which Shakespeare's texts and their putative original context can mount against the creative thrust of each new generation will be fairly limited. After all, people have to live their own lives and see things their own way, and they have to do so in the times and places in which they find themselves. Shakespeare himself would perfectly understand this, and he treated his own sources, highly revered though some of them were, with a no less cavalier opportunism.

In any case, what did Shakespeare really *mean* to write? The scholarly attempt to provide a single definitive text embodying as near as possible the author's intention – a foundational goal for literary studies – is nowadays widely seen as the speculative undertaking it really is. When readings seem doubtful, editors of Shakespeare have traditionally chosen between the variants, or made emendations, being guided by their own historical and philological knowledge and literary sensitivity. Although such scholarship ultimately underlies every reader's necessary attempt to interpret the plays in the Shakespearian context, the learned guesswork will never come to an end. The historic policy decision embodied in the new Oxford edition of *King Lear* is merely to keep the quarto and folio versions separate, since the conflations proposed by editors from the eighteenth century onwards resulted in mongrel texts which could not possibly correspond to Shakespeare's full intention at any given time. The Oxford editor is still free to come up with fresh emendations to both versions.

One theory is that Shakespeare himself re-shaped *King Lear* for a transfer to the Blackfriars indoor theatre (Taylor 1983). Be that as it may, subsequent revivals and editions have adapted his plays to new circumstances in ways still more radical, for it was beyond the scope of language to prevent this. Even more strikingly than most other human beings, Shakespeare was immediately dispossessed of his words. Except in a trivial sense, texts do not exist on paper but in people's heads, and the stability of a classic text is inversely proportional to its hold on the folk imagination. This paradox applies to Shakespeare not only within non-English traditions, where translations usually serve as the medium, but in England, where his plays appeared in botched-up pirated versions from the very start, and have ever since been repeatedly cut, extended or otherwise adapted, by acting companies, scholars and publishers. Characters and scenes have been completely removed, characters and scenes have been added or reintroduced, tragic endings have been made happy, bawdry has been bowdlerized, and doubtful or aesthetically unpleasing readings have been emended. Although in English traditions people often remember particular phrases and whole speeches, there is no guarantee that every single word was Shakespeare's, and people can always compound the 'corruption' by misremembering the texts which do happen to be available.

Much of what they remember is in any case not a matter of verbal detail but of stories, characters, and visual impressions of particular performances. In short, the cultural history of a classic text is strongly analogous to oral transmission, involving a dynamic interaction with successive contexts of use, and the corresponding liability to textual change and re-interpretation. The great classic texts have not so much cowed their users into servile deference, as offered a stimulus to joyous self-discovery.

One of the first practical consequences of these observations for the teaching of Shakespeare is that it no longer matters quite so much whether all the students in a class use one and the same edition – the 'set text'. Perhaps teachers should even encourage students to borrow or buy various editions, so that notions of textual authority can be undermined by classroom discussions of the readings of different editors. For similar reasons, teachers need to have a modest conception of their own role. Even less than editors, they are not custodians of Shakespeare. Shakespeare is not something which belongs to the human race in the abstract, and which teachers have to protect from contamination or theft. Shakespeare is for everybody to do what they want to with. In particular here, Shakespeare is for students, students in any place at any time. He is theirs at least as much as he is anybody else's, and ideally their relations with him should be as free and easy, as hedonistic, as selfish, as wilful, as much influenced by the whirligig of fashion, as their relations with, say, film stars or pop groups.

One of the topics suggested in *The Dolphin*'s invitation to contributors for the present issue was: 'The question of literary studies ("reading books") as a somewhat anachronistic academic exercise *vis a vis* media or cultural studies'. My own experience is that by rejecting bardolatry and authoritarian notions of the 'correct' interpretation I am able to hint that Shakespeare may be a live cultural potential for the present. If the classics are still to speak to each new generation, they must be deprived of – *rescued* from – their aura of privilege, which prevents them from competing on equal terms with the mass culture of the here and now. This does not mean that they – and other texts, rediscovered or new – will cease to exist as classics, or that the canon will fade away. Nor does it mean that readers must stop trying to relate them to their putative original contexts as a way of working out what their authors actually meant. That, on the contrary, is the only way to read, and as teachers we must always help our students to get on with it. The point is merely that literary activity minimally involves at least two parties, a sender and a receiver, the former often dead and buried, the latter always alive, and that both of them are entitled to a certain respect. Like human interaction in general, reading thrives best under conditions of unconstrained equality.

2. Educational contexts

So much for literary pragmatics and the successive contextualizations and uses made of Shakespeare. But how does one embody the pragmatic insights in a programme of study for undergraduates? – that is, for students who are not necessarily going to carry out literary pragmatic research. How does one actually plan a series of ordinary classes on Shakespeare?

This last question is misleading in its present form, since it implies that a Shakespeare course can be the same the world over. The first step in any kind of educational planning is to take into account the full circumstances on which the proposed educational measures are going to impinge. In matters of language *education,* in other words, the contextual dimensions of linguistic and literary activity actually become even more important. For me to claim that my own department's practices in literature teaching could be straightforwardly replicated somewhere else would be not only bad pragmatics but bad pedagogics, and the claim would be equally foolhardy coming from any other English teacher in any other situation.

This does not mean that English teachers working under different conditions should not talk to each other. Sometimes not everything about two situations will be different; the students may be roughly at the same age and level of maturity, or some of the aims of the two programmes may be similar. Also, initiatives such as *The Dolphin*'s in providing a forum for the present discussion will probably make us more self-conscious about what we are doing, precisely because we shall start to compare and contrast the configuration of human and institutional variables in our own situation with those obtaining in other educational set-ups. The contrastive study of English Studies is already becoming a growth area in its own right (see Dodsworth 1989; Sell 1989), and this bodes well for our students.

At first blush it might seem that the most important human variable is us, the teachers. As people we are certainly all different, which means that we bring different things to the subject. We also live in several different societies and our own experience of English varies widely. Some of us are more grounded in British English, others in American or Australian or Indian English, and these are only the most obvious of our biases. All the same, we do form a kind of community. We have already studied Shakespeare and the English tradition, for instance, and would be likely to leaf through a copy of *The Dolphin.* This arguably makes us far more like each other than the typical freshman student in one society is like the typical freshman student in another.

All human beings are born with pretty much the same physiological and mental abilities; there is no reason in nature why most people should not produce and perceive more or less the same noises, and also process things in much the same way. That our students do not do always do this in English is because they are still culturally differentiated, by the timing and extent of their immersion in both English and other languages.

One of the paradoxes here is that some non-native speakers of English eventually come to have a deeper native feel for English literature than many native speakers, and as we have seen they also bring to bear contextualizing perspectives which are not open to even a fully acculturated native speaker. Again, for the average non-native learner, reading Shakespeare may feel a good deal less problematic than for a native learner, because there are fewer linguistic and sociocultural *faux amis*. To put it this way is to relapse into the discussion of right and wrong ways of interpreting stable authorial meaning when in fact, even from the start, there could have been only a linguistic and sociocultural agreement about what Shakespeare meant, and we can never relive that putative consensus. To repeat: all we can hope to achieve is agreement about what the Elizabethans and Jacobeans agreed. All the same, in these deliberations the native English learner is certainly more impeded than the non-native by current linguistic and sociocultural agreements as to how English works at present. To turn this round the other way, one sign of an EFL teacher's success may be when the students begin to find Shakespeare *more* difficult. It may show that they are becoming conscious of the differences between earlier and contemporary English praxis.

As for the institutional variables in the teaching situation, this is a matter of educational aims, of syllabus planning, of facilities, of teaching formats, of administrative structure, of tradition. In any institution these considerations amount to a pattern of possibilities and limitations that will be peculiar to that institution and fundamentally affect the way English is treated. Their influence is all the more powerful in that, unless we frequently visit and have worked in English departments elsewhere, we probably give such things very little thought. The case for professional mobility is really very strong.

3. One particular educational situation

With what kind of students, then, and under what educational circumstances, do I myself at present work on Shakespeare?

Of Finland's five million inhabitants six percent are Swedish speakers, who mainly live in three coastal areas: in the Helsingfors (in Finnish: Helsinki) region; in the Åbo (in Finnish: Turku) region and the Åland Islands; and in Ostrobothnia. Those living in the Helsingfors and Åbo areas tend to be very fluent in Finnish or completely bilingual, whereas those from Ostrobothnia are sometimes rather weaker in Finnish, and Ålanders weaker still. There is a fully developed Swedish educational system, of which Åbo Akademi, founded in 1918, the year after Independence, represents the university level. It is a major international research centre, and has six faculties with a student body of some 5,000. The English Department has an annual undergraduate intake of 35 students, some 80% of them with Swedish as their mother tongue, the remainder being Finnish speakers and foreigners.

When they start their studies most students have read hardly any English literature, and their knowledge of literature from Swedish Finland, Finland and Sweden is also more limited than, say, their British counterpart's knowledge of English literature. All the same, they have usually had eight or nine years of English at school and they have to be fairly good at it: every year we cream off our 35 freshmen from 150-200 applicants. Their general education is actually far broader than most British schools offer, usually including four or five languages, and they have a certain roundedness and maturity in other ways as well. Normally entering university at 19 or 20, some of them have already spent a year abroad, and the lamentably few men among them have sometimes already done military service or the civilian alternative. Again, although their life-style as students is by no means without its fun and games, they do tend to shoulder certain responsibilities. There are no university fees to pay, and students get a modest government grant, but the Finnish cost of living is extremely high, so that rather than accumulating huge debts they usually take on part-time work and summer jobs, often acquiring experience and developing contacts which are of direct benefit to them in their subsequent careers. Some of them also live in stable sexual relationships and have children (for whom day-care is available). Their general level of purposeful determination reflects both the high value placed on education in Finnish society as whole and a widespread faith in the Finnish educational system. A recent Reader's Digest survey discovered that, whereas six in ten Britons think their own country's educational system is the worst in Europe, most Finns rank theirs as best. Even during the late sixties Finland did not have much student unrest.

Undergraduates in the humanities work towards a master's degree which on average takes them six or seven years, culminating with a fairly substantial thesis. It is a combined honours degree, with language students taking:

20 credits in obligatory General Studies (i.e. theory of knowledge, data processing, Swedish or Finnish (whichever is not their mother tongue), a foreign language, General Linguistics, Phonetics, Latin, and a contrastive approach to Swedish grammar);

80 credits in their main subject;

40 credits in their first subsidiary subject;

and **20 credits** in a second subsidiary subject or spread over several subjects.

Some of the subjects often taken together with English are: Finnish, German, Russian, French, General Linguistics, Comparative Literature, Art History. Trainee teachers take a further 20 credits in Education.

At worst, the range of different subjects studied is fragmenting and demotivating, especially since most subjects are further broken up into an array of small courses, each with its own examination. At best, though, and in combination with the students' basic maturity and sense of responsibility, it makes for a high level of well-informed and serious discussion. Students do not study one subject at a time, but several simultaneously, and this makes further demands on their self-reliance, since in the event of timetabling clashes between two departments they have to manage partly by means of private study – regular attendance at courses is not compulsory in most humanities subjects.

Visitors to the English department sometimes comment on the friendly atmosphere. Students and staff are on Christian-name terms, and there is a certain *esprit de corps* which is focused through the English language itself. Several staff members are native English speakers, all teaching takes place in English, and so do the planning and decision-making of the official Departmental Council, in which students have half the places and full voting rights. There is a departmental magazine to which students and staff contribute poems, stories, news and views in English, and a student society – Britannica – which puts on plays and organizes other cultural events and parties, all in English. The department also has a network of contacts with English-speaking countries. Every year some students do voluntary social work in Britain, and some of them study for fully exchangeable credits in English at Sheffield University, with which Åbo Akademi is twinned, and from which our department receives undergraduate and postgraduate students of English.

There are three lines of study in the English Department: a general line; a line for trainee teachers; and a line which trains language experts for international business. This last line is highly specialized and I shall say no more about it here. The only difference between the teachers' line and the general line is that the former includes an obligatory course on applied linguistics with speech and drama in the fourth year. In their fifth and sixth years, English majors attend seminars and write degree essays and a master's thesis within any area of the subject – philology, linguistics, applied linguistics, English and American literature, British and American society. In their fourth year they do a number of options, either in our own department or in an English department elsewhere. In their first three years students do a core curriculum in English which gives the 40 credits required for a first subsidiary subject. Shakespeare can be studied in fourth-year courses or as a thesis topic, but the Shakespeare course which I shall soon be describing is an integral part of this core curriculum, which is why I cannot discuss it in complete isolation from the rest.

In planning the core curriculum we have been strongly influenced by the confluence of pragmatic and pedagogical considerations mentioned earlier, and all the more so because we wished to counteract the tendency of the entire degree structure towards a confusing and demotivating fragmentation. At least within English, we wanted to guarantee that there would be larger rather than smaller courses, and only occasional exams instead of an endless hurdle-race of them. In the interdisciplinary spirit of literary pragmatics, we see the three main types of thing studied – language, literature and society – as capable of mutually contextualizing each other, and we deal with them simultaneously, with as much interconnection as possible. Students' spoken and written proficiency in English is developed in the same synergetic spirit, by exercising it on the actual topics they happen to be studying in English; students produce for class discussion a graduated sequence of essays on all areas of the subject, including interdisciplinary aspects of it. And we try to ensure the coherence of the entire set-up by teaching each of the three big core curriculum courses as a team of teachers working in close cooperation.

In the first-year course students study language, literature and society during the past twenty years. In the second year they do the same for the period 500-1660, and in the third year for 1660 to the present. Throughout, the main foci are Britain and North America. And Shakespeare comes in the spring term of the second year.

4. Contextualized and contextualizing Shakespeare teaching

The aims of the Shakespeare classes are inseparable from the overall aims of the second-year course as a whole. The proficiency aim is to develop reading, written and spoken proficiency in English through the study and active discussion of the history of the English language, literature and society. For our present purpose, other salient aims can be grouped as follows:

Aims relevant to the Shakespearian context

To develop an understanding of political, social, cultural and ideological trends in the period;

to develop a sense of the interrelationships between the English language, English literature and sociocultural contexts and of related sociolinguistic considerations;

to develop a philological grasp of points of vocabulary, phonology, spelling, accidence, syntax and semantics;

to develop a grasp both of the development of literary styles and genres during the period, and of sociological and biographical aspects of literary production and reception.

To gain some sense of the way in which the reception of literary works from this period has changed over the centuries down to the present.

In this last connection, I should also emphasize that the course is based on the assumption that Shakespeare is, or can become, a live potential for students' own intellectual and cultural life. Another way of saying this is that the course aims to break down the distinction between work and play, between curricular and extra-curricular. This is much easier to do with a classic drama than with a classic novel or poem, since students can start their interaction with it by acting a scene or two during class time. This in itself is a fun thing to do and already brings the class together as a community around Shakespeare. If the course is successful, things will start to happen outside of class as well.

Because the students are simultaneously doing courses in other departments, the Shakespeare component cannot be too ambitious in its scope. An in-depth experience is in any case better than a superficial survey at this stage in their development. So each year the course concentrates on only two major plays, preferably not too long, and in different genres, a frequent pairing being *Twelfth Night* and *Macbeth*. As already explained, students are not all asked to get one and the same edition of the plays. There are many inexpensive paperback editions of Shakespeare, all of which give valuable help with the Shakespearian context, and the differences between their texts can be used in class to loosen up notions of an authoritative version.

By the spring term of their second year, students have still not read very widely in the literature of their mother tongue, and cannot be expected to have a strong sense of the role of Shakespeare within Finland-Swedish culture. On the other hand, they have now spent two terms on British and American language, literature and society of the past twenty years, and in the autumn term of the second year they have worked forward in the interdisciplinary study of English language, literature and society from 500 to 1485. The Shakespeare sessions, which begin when they have already begun to get some feel for the Renaissance, continue for a six-week period over the middle of term. During this time students spend six hours a week in Shakespeare classes, and tutorials and lectures on other parts of the English syllabus are suspended. The reasons for this intense concentration are partly that Shakespeare is regarded as centrally important for the entire second-year course, but also that his plays can be more effectively presented in a shorter rather than a longer time. This is a matter of trying to simulate and sustain some sort of theatrical excitement. If the study of a play is spread out over two or three months, it goes flat and will never become a part of students' lives.

A key element in our arrangements for Shakespeare is 'Department Time'. In the official departmental programme, this is the label we have given to a two-hour slot on Wednesday afternoons. During Department Time various forms of activity take place which are not part of the regular teaching, but which nevertheless have a bearing on the subject, and on the general life and atmosphere of the Department. Not only meetings of the official Departmental Council are scheduled at this time, but also guest lectures, debates, video shows, travel reports, poetry readings, and so on. In other words Department Time is part of our general strategy for eroding the boundaries between work and play, and offers the ideal opportunity for video shows of the Shakespeare plays being studied. We do not follow the videos up with formal discussions of them, since we hope that students will discuss them among themselves, just as they would with any other film which they have been to see; Shakespeare has to compete with other forms of entertainment in an unprivileged and unpressurizing way. Another point of policy is that videos of the plays are always shown *before* students have begun to work on them in detail. This means that when students start to wrestle with philological problems, they already know that there is 'a way through' and that the play can actually be performed by twentieth-century actors. In principle the same thing can of course happen in an English-speaking culture: not everybody reads a Shakespeare play before seeing it performed. And in enabling the students' first experience of a play to take this form we have again opted for the least pressurizing approach. One sign of its effectiveness is that at some later stage students often express a desire to see the same video again. But although we naturally comply with this, we would also hope to expose them to other productions as well. No single production is more authoritative than any other, just as no text or critical interpretation is.

Department Time can also be used for other Shakespeare-related activities: listening to readings of the sonnets, acting particular scenes, and so on. But in order to squeeze in enough actual teaching hours, on a few occasions we also have to use Department Time for regular Shakespeare classes. If this further confuses the distinction between work and play, it is all to the good.

Over and above Department Time activities, six hours are devoted to introductory lectures designed to illuminate particular aspects of the Shakespearian context. Social and political history do not need to be dealt with, since this is taken care of within the second-year course's regular history component, taught by another member of the second-year team. Rather, the lectures offer: a survey of pre-Shakespearian drama, and of the rise of the acting profession and of public and private playhouses; a brief sketch of Shakespeare's life; a few words on his sources; some general remarks on his use of verse and prose; and a contrastive account of Shakespeare's English (early-Modern vs. present-day English), which links up with the second year philology component, taught by another colleague. Students receive a handout of 10-15 pages, containing illustrations of theatres, a list of the Shakespeare canon, a list of all the major differences between Shakespearian and modern

English, and illustrations of the differences between early and late Shakespearian blank verse.

After this preparation, a total of 22 hours are assigned to classwork with a group of about 15 students. One two-hour session is devoted to each of the five acts of both plays studied, and there is a two-hour final discussion.

The type of work done in the classes assumes that students have already worked on the language of the plays, though in one or two of the early sessions they are asked to do some philological gobbet exercises just to make sure. The basic mode of discussion follows a question and answer pattern, but as teacher I am trying, not so much to find out what the students know, as to ask the sort of question which will make them think and bring the play alive. The students themselves also ask questions, both of their colleagues and of myself, as a way of comparing their own difficulties or impressions or interpretations with those of other people. The gap between one question and the next can of course vary in length; sometimes discussion runs on fruitfully with very few questions indeed. Particularly as students gain self-confidence and become more interested, they are eager to volunteer observations of their own, and in Finland there is never a risk that students will talk just for the sake of talking, not only because they are mature in the way already outlined, but because there is a deep-seated taboo against small talk and waffle. At best their remarks carry so much weight that I regard them as the single most important input to the educational process, and the other side of the coin is that students expect a high level of common sense and illumination from the teacher. *The Dolphin*'s terms of reference for the present issue include the question, 'How did you strike the pedagogical balance (if any) between a "teacherly" and "masterminding" containment of the progression of the seminar and the potential anarchy of active student participation in, say, setting up agendas for the class discussions?' In saying that no interpretation is more authoritative than any other I am not saying that anything goes; an interpretation still has to be argued for according to generally accepted criteria for rational discussion. But students do not necessarily find such criteria unpalatable, and in my view the teacher's job is actually to work towards an atmosphere of mutual respect on all sides. The way to do this is precisely by being for ever open to discussion, and by trying, as unofficiously and undemonstratively as possible, to exemplify and encourage a high standard of debate.

Some of the classwork is a matter of comparing how various participants relate the text to the Shakespearian context. It is historical, philological, hermeneutic, in other words. But most discussion is in effect about how Shakespeare is contextualizable in late-twentieth-century Britain and Finland. I myself sometimes refer to well-known earlier interpretations by actors, directors and critics within the British tradition, and I also allow myself frequent 'Ooohs!' and 'Ahs!'. That is to say: during a discussion of the story, or the characters, or staging potentialities, or structure, or particular phrases, I will make remarks that are frankly exclamatory. Without very much analyzing my response or the textual stimulus to it, I simply make clear that I am moved or excited by something, and perhaps also reveal that I personally have found a particular line or speech worth memorizing. It is a pedagogical technique I have copied partly from Addison's singling out of the 'beauties' of *Paradise Lost* and from Arnold's 'touchstones', but I was also lucky enough to have several teachers at school who did the same sort of thing. I believe students need a chance to observe such models of response in action, since it can spur them on to react for themselves. The crucial thing is not so much the precise nature of my response, as the fact that I have a response at all, and that it is alive and important to me personally. Given my own roots, it is a response representative of the target culture, but the target culture, we have seen, is not to be privileged, and I am not aiming at some absurdly neo-colonialist encroachment upon students' freedom. Though many students may at first lean on me for a kind of vicarious enjoyment of Shakespeare, that is a better start than no start at all, and is probably the way most native students of an author get going as well. More important, students soon begin to find 'buzz-spots' of their own, sometimes in agreement with me, sometimes definitely not, and I complement my own 'Ooohs!' and 'Ahs!' by trying to draw out such knowledge as they have of Shakespeare's role in their own culture, and by hinting at ways in which they could extend it.

In this connection I have contemplated some sort of cooperation with the Department of Comparative Literature, since it is they who deal with Scandinavian literature, and their present professor, as noted, is a distinguished translator of Shakespeare. The main obstacle is the shortage of time and the pressure of work in the students' other courses, and for the same reasons I cannot at this level start to put students in E-mail contact with students in other countries. This is something I am hoping to do with students at a later stage, as part of a literary pragmatic experiment in cross-cultural teaching. Students will be able to write master's theses comparing and contrasting their own use of Shakespeare with that of students in Britain and Taiwan, one of the main educational aims being the development of cultural self-consciousness and tolerance.

The other thing that happens in the second-year Shakespeare classes is of course that both the students and I myself ham the lines. When I do it, it is a way for me to actualize certain interpretations, and again to suggest a live response, in what is the most natural and economical way. When students do it, it gives me insight into the way they are interpreting. Fortunately they are sufficiently well-motivated not to mind being corrected on points of intonation and pronunciation, but I try to place most emphasis on questions such as 'What would you say is the climax of this speech?' or 'How does the rhythm of this speech seem to differ from the rhythm of that one?'

In the final class, we have a general discussion of both plays studied, and students explain how they are planning to write their essays. Of the twelve essays required for the second-year core-syllabus course, one or two have to be on Shakespeare. They must be typewritten and of about five or six pages in length, but at this stage we do not require that there should be a formal scholarly apparatus with footnotes and bibliography. The main idea is that students should develop, in an articulate and well-ordered manner, their own views on a topic of their own choice: I explain that I shall be very bored if they simply regurgitate my wisdom, and in fact there is little risk of this. For many students the main problem is that, having spent six weeks working on two plays such as *Twelfth Night* and *Macbeth* in the way already described, they are so full of ideas that they find the scope of a short essay too restrictive. If, as sometimes happens, they write something of altogether larger proportions, it can upset the rhythm of their essay-writing for the second year course as a whole, though as teachers we can also allow one major piece of work to count as more than one essay. At all events, the final Shakespeare class is often a useful exercise in defining a topic and planning its presentation. If they so wish, students also have a chance to re-draft their work after one-to-one feedback from me during my reception hours. This process-writing approach, as long as it does not prevent their steady movement through the syllabus, is something the department wishes to encourage. But even without re-drafting, the essays produced often make interesting reading.

The completed essay-work on Shakespeare is graded, and this grade is combined with grades from the other second-year essays. There is also a final four-hour examination for the entire second-year course, and a *viva voce* examination for students whose overall grade for the course falls on a borderline.

From what I have said earlier it follows that such formal measures give only a partial idea of whether the Shakespeare teaching has succeeded. As a literary pragmaticist, I hope to see two things happening as a result of my Shakespeare teaching: in the first place, that students make informed guesses as to the texts' original meaning and force within the putative Shakespearian context; but no less importantly, that they take possession of Shakespeare and recontextualize him for themselves. The department's strong English ethos, with the blurred boundaries between work and play, is conducive to this. One of my memories of greatest job satisfaction is of the Britannica Society getting together to write and stage their own hilarious parody of *Macbeth*.

Teaching Shakespeare in the Nineties

Niels Bugge Hansen, University of Copenhagen, Denmark

For Shakespeare, the nineties were a decade of growth and experimentation – the 1590s, that is. There are clear signs all around that the 1990s will be, as were the previous decades, a boom period for the Shakespeare business. The academic exploitation of the seemingly inexhaustible field of Shakespearean ore goes hand in hand with a lively interest, shared by producers and audiences, in stage presentations of Shakespeare's plays. Imaginative, spectacular, and experimental versions are on show throughout the world, Denmark being no exception. Each theatre season provides a new spate of productions, often in new, lively translations that help us forget that Shakespeare is not our contemporary. And in recent years Danish audiences have also been given increasing opportunities to come to grips with Shakespeare's words in the original, through films and videotapes as well as through visits by travelling companies to our native stages, at Elsinore and elsewhere. Not to mention the increasing number of theatre buffs and ordinary tourists who have found their way to the National Theatre, the Barbican and the Royal Shakespeare for breathtaking performances by outstanding directors and actors.

Meanwhile, the scholars and critics keep up the steam in the world-wide industry of writing about Shakespeare, each year adding an overwhelming and bewildering pile of books and articles. At the same time these academics, along with thousands of humbler colleagues in schools and universities all over the world, are engaged in the parallel industry of teaching Shakespeare; all charged with the awesome task of conveying at the same time understanding and enthusiasm, critical acumen and thrilling experience. These years more and more students in our secondary schools are offered the opportunity to study Shakespeare, more and more teachers are faced with the challenge of making that encounter a worthwhile effort. How should they prepare themselves for that task? How should we who are in charge of Shakespeare courses in the universities prepare future teachers (and ourselves) for that task? It makes good sense to stop and consider what we are doing and what we should be doing. Are the courses we taught 20 years ago, or the courses we attended 30 years ago, right for the 90s? The ideas on this subject which I offer here grow out of a Shakespeare course I taught recently in the English Department at Copenhagen University. My essay deals with the plans I had for that course and with my plans for my next course on Shakespeare on the basis of past experiences, but it also deals with the actual seminar. It outlines ideal conditions, but does not, however, ignore or conceal the adjustments and compromises, complications and frustrations that are part of real life in the classroom.

One basic assumption for the seminar I have in mind is that the students, for all their differences, share as a minimum background a first-year survey course including one Shakespeare play. Another is that for the majority this may well be their final exposure to Shakespeare in the classroom before they go on to a variety of unpredictable careers. Given those conditions, how do we make the best possible use of 14 two-hour periods in the course of one semester? What are the objectives? I am not going to argue the value of literary studies as such. I assume that all the students in the class committed themselves to that belief when they chose to come to an arts faculty. Nor am I going here to argue the value and relevance of studying Shakespeare. The question is: how should we set about it?

In the past my colleagues and I have often devoted a whole semester to the study of one play. The advantages of that choice are obvious: the detailed attention to the complexities of Shakespeare's text yields both language acquisition in a historical dimension and literary appreciation of diction, character, structure, dramatic strategies, etc. There is time for lectures on context and background, the development of drama and theatres, and aspects of Shakespearean scholarship (dating, sources, editorial problems); and the availability of critical literature about the play (casebooks, etc.) offers ample opportunity for studies in applied criticism. The methodological benefits are apparent. The course works as a *vademecum* for further exploration in the Shakespeare canon, whether in other classes or privately undertaken.

The true value of this model rests on the assumption that it is in fact followed by further exploration. Otherwise the student goes out into the world with a rather narrow conception of and familiarity with England's chief contribution to world literature. If we could be sure that the assumption is correct, all is well, but ...

As a variation on this procedure I and others have offered courses that combined focus on one play with a more cursory study of related plays. Such clusters of, typically, four plays might be: mature comedies, problem plays, great tragedies, histories, late plays. Clearly this gives a wider scope to the student's knowledge of Shakespeare, but still a somewhat biassed impression of what the playwright has to offer. Is it the best of two worlds, or does it leave us fallen between two stools?

A recent stay in the USA as an exchange professor (at the University of Iowa) gave me a chance to try out different approaches. I was asked to teach one of their standard courses at intermediate undergraduate level. The idea of this course is to introduce the students to a wide and varied selection of Shakespeare's plays. (They can then progress to more thorough studies of selected plays at a later stage). In this course they read about a dozen plays in as many weeks, with three weekly hours (either 2 x 1½ hours or 3 x 1 hour). The primary objective is that they should read and get to know the plays. The pace is obviously somewhat hectic, but the reading habits of the average American college student and the system's built-in measures of checking reading and comprehension seem to ensure that they actually read the texts from week to week. The long-term benefits of such rapid and almost inevitably superficial reading are another matter.

On my return I decided to experiment with a modified version of this type of course. My incentives to do so were the merits of the American course and the desire to offer Danish students of English a broadly based introduction to Shakespeare's plays, useful for students at different levels in our degree programme. This way they would get a basic all-round idea of Shakespeare's dramatic achievements. I launched the course with the following title and course description:

SHAKESPEARE – A WRITER'S PROGRESS
This course offers a survey of Shakespeare's dramatic career, the stages in his development as well as his contributions in the various categories of plays: comedies, tragedies, and histories. The course centres on a study of five major plays: *Romeo and Juliet, Twelfth Night, Richard 11, Othello* and *The Tempest*. The dramatic qualities of the texts will be emphasized, and videotapes will be included in the classwork. Besides the texts in annotated editions (the *New Penguin Shakespeare* series is recommended) the reading comprises Philip Edwards, *Shakespeare: A Writer's Progress*.

The course was meant to tie in with an excursion to Stratford half way through the semester, but less than half the members of this class took part in the trip. Once the RSC repertoire was known, this entailed a few changes in the choice of plays and the order in which they were studied. *Twelfth Night* was replaced by *Much Ado* and *Othello* by *King Lear*. These two plays started the course, and *King Lear* in particular got the lion's share of the classes. This did not, however, essentially change my aims and procedures. Attendance stabilized itself around 20, subject to the fluctuations we always have to take into account. The number suited my procedures quite well.

The choice of secondary material, Philip Edwards's *Shakespeare: A Writer's Progress* (1987), which gave me my course title, proved a happy one, I think. It is an OPUS book, fairly inexpensive, easily available, and comprising about 180 pages written in a very accessible style. Introductions to Shakespeare come and go; for my next course it may well be out of print. If not, I'd be ready to use it once more. It seems closer to my needs than, say, Germaine Greer's *Shakespeare* (1986) in the OUP Past Masters Series, also a fine little introduction, but based on aspects of Shakespeare's ideas (poetics, ethics, politics, etc.), whereas Edwards approaches the plays by genre divisions, headed by a brief survey of Shakespeare's career and an essay on relationships, an approach that clearly cuts across the genre boundaries. As we progressed through the semester and the genres, students were asked to read chapters in Edwards. It gave useful background and perspective. It could be referred to and taken for granted, but did not require (or, at least, get) special attention, and did not divert our attention from our primary object of study – the play texts. I did not expect or encourage much other further reading in the semester, but for those who needed it I referred to the Penguin editions' suggestions (plus casebooks) for the individual plays. I also gave them a list of books of a more general nature.

Like Edwards's, my emphasis was not on contexts (life, theatres) or scholarly problems like sources, dating, editing, etc., but on the plays as scripts that use dramatic conventions and live and generate meaning in the reader's mind and in the theatre. Lectures (which rarely exceeded 30 minutes) were chiefly on the history and the distinguishing features of genres – referring to our *Glossary of Literary Terms* (M.H. Abrams's, that is), and with considerable debt to Northrop Frye – and Aristotle.

With a syllabus of five plays in a course of 14 90-minute sessions the schedule is tight. To include as many different approaches and procedures as possible I tried to vary our 'method' from play to play.

The declared emphasis on the dramatic qualities of the texts was realized in our study of *Much Ado*, our first play. Theoretically, this was to be by reference to a short, but excellent opening chapter in J. R. Mulryne's little book on the play (Mulryne 1865), which stresses the page/stage contrast and the need to read with visual imagination, especially comedies; in practice, it was done by asking volunteers to prepare and perform in the classroom the two scenes where Benedick and Beatrice are 'baited'. In the past I have, of course, had students read parts, but this, irrespective of talent, is so much more rewarding in opening everybody's eyes to the importance of pace, blocking, asides, mute play, etc. The questions posed in the preparation of the acting and the comments elicited by the viewing foster enjoyment and stimulate critical thought. Acting in the classroom is not offered as a revolutionizing idea; but it is, I believe, hard to overemphasize the value of this 'dramatic' approach in one way or another as a component in any course on Shakespeare – or any drama course for that matter. One clear advantage of this device is that it tends to break down the reservations and hesitations less advanced students may have about speaking in an academic discussion.

As a less enterprising attempt in the same direction I had first asked students, in preparing for the class, to 'choose four or five short passages (1-6 lines each), which in your opinion contribute substantially to the overall picture of a particular character. Not necessarily lines spoken by that character. Be prepared to speak them in character and to explain why you chose them'. This proved a very productive approach to the initial discussion of 'character'.

In recent years, videos have added greatly to the dissemination of exposure to Shakespeare. This is indubitably a great advantage for the study of his plays. In connection with this course I made it possible for interested students to view screen productions of several of the plays in our syllabus, but not during classes. To make videotapes educationally worthwhile in our short, precious time, the viewing needs to be planned, structured, and guided. In our study of *King Lear* I used selected scenes from two films (Lawrence Olivier and Michael Hordern respectively playing Lear). This comparative approach yielded good ways of discussing setting, costume, character, mood, in short all the choices that have been made, and which lead you back to the text. This is relevant – and at the same time comfortable for the teacher who never took a course in film analysis!

One obvious weakness of a course that spans so much is that depth is sacrificed at the altar of breadth. There is no guarantee that the students' reading has made them come to grips, line by line, with the intricacies, the subtleties, the difficulties of the text. Rather, it is pretty certain most of them haven't. There is, I believe, no satisfactory solution to this. You can hope (and perhaps effect) that in wide-ranging discussions on character and theme, the need for scrutiny, for detailed attention to lines of text and their meaning, arises and is demonstrated from time to time. You can, of course, also select sample passages or key passages for the purpose. I decided to try to kill several birds with one stone by asking students to compare three Danish translations (by Foersom, Lembcke, and Østergaard) of *King Lear*, II.iv. 263-70 ('O, reason not the need ...'), and to translate the following seven lines (271-77) into Danish blank verse, and then to 'write a comment on the whole speech, explaining Lear's situation, i.e. his state of mind and the circumstances that have given rise to it'. This took some of the close-reading exercise out of the classroom, but the translations were of course discussed in a session.

The nature of the course, i.e. chiefly the bulk of the reading, made me reluctant to ask for much writing. Likewise, individual assignments for oral presentation were very limited in number, partly for this reason, partly because it was hard to fit them into the tight schedule. The larger issues, in *King Lear* and in the plays generally, were handled in discussions growing out of the lecture sections on genre, applying general and abstract statement to individual texts and singling out distinctive features.

When we proceeded from *King Lear* to *Romeo and Juliet*, it was an obvious choice to approach the latter in terms of genre, noting differences as well as similarities between early and mature tragedy. At the same time *Romeo and Juliet* provided an opportunity to examine tragic form vis-a-vis comic form.

It also served to bring in Shakespeare's poetic language (Edwards has a good chapter on 'Poems and Poetry') and issues of dramatizing narrative material. Extracts from Brooke's narrative poem on *Romeus and Juliet* (the chief source) were distributed, but, as it happened, dealt with in a rather cursory and desultory manner. Here obvious opportunities for written and oral assignments were wasted for lack of time.

There is no denying that time is a major problem to grapple with in this type of course. The histories, represented by *Richard II*, were the chief victims of this condition. For this play some historical background provided by the teacher was deemed necessary, but otherwise genre considerations again gave us the entry. Similarities and differences between tragedy and history were considered in lecture form, and students who had returned from the excursion to Stratford shared their impressions of Marlowe's *Edward II* with the others. Students were directed to examine structure and imagery, with reference to secondary material, especially Richard Altick's fine article on symphonic imagery in the play (Altick 1947).

When we got to our last play, *The Tempest*, we benefited from the fact that the play was running at one of the Copenhagen theatres. This provided a welcome focus for discussion. Otherwise I will restrict my comments here to a list of work points intended for preparation and class discussion. A student might in class be asked to address himself to one of these points, but such presentations were not assigned beforehand. The questions could of course equally well serve as essay topics or short lectures proper.

WORK POINTS
1 What support do you find for calling the play a comedy?
2 Why does Prospero treat Ferdinand so unkindly?
3 What is the point of the play within the play?
4 Who is the most important character in the play – and why?
5 What is the main theme in the play? What do you base your opinion on?
6 What functions does Caliban play with regard to the play's plot and themes?
7 What functions does Gonzalo serve with regard to the play's plot and themes?
8 Why does Prospero break his staff and drown his book?
9 What significance do you see in the epilogue?

This article is written from hindsight. It is a report of a seminar that has taken place. The scenario was substantially realized as it was intended. Some, at least, of the weaknesses and shortcomings have been laid open. An anonymous evaluation half way through the semester revealed no consistent or serious dissatisfaction with the chosen plan, on the contrary. (The evaluation was not my idea. It was a faculty-wide experiment that semester with a standard questionnaire). I hope to offer a similar Shakespeare course again before long. I do believe its assets outweigh its deficiencies. It achieves its objective of providing an all-round introduction to Shakespearean drama in a historical context, relating the plays to the history of dramatic forms rather than their social and cultural contexts. It touches on a wide range of issues in and approaches to Shakespearean drama. It addresses itself to the respective merits of being face to face with the plays in the study and on the stage. It is interesting and inspiring to teach, more so than the narrowly defined one-play course. It is also, I believe, more interesting and inspiring to attend. The student who has taken it has, hopefully, had enjoyable reading experiences and faced challenging ideas and questions. And if it falls to his lot to teach Shakespeare, he has, I'd like to hope, a variety of notions about how to do it that he can draw upon.

What would I like to change to improve the value of the course? I would like to devise ways of conducting better class discussions (not group discussions). By this I mean discussions everybody can't help taking part in, discussions that develop spontaneously, yet end where they are meant to. And I would like to involve and activate every student through written work which I can not only suggest but actually demand as his share of a mutual obligation. I return to my starting point, the inspiration I drew from my teaching in the USA. I do not wish to imitate the American emphasis on quizzes and tests, but our education system has come to look more and more like theirs in recent years, and there are classroom procedures, especially in evaluating, that we might well, in everybody's interests, adopt.

As marking and grading become a more and more onerous and time-consuming task, I'd like to end by briefly mentioning a test for basic literary comprehension I was introduced to by a colleague at University of Iowa, Professor John F. Huntley. In his essay 'An Objective Test for Literary Comprehension' (Huntley 1977) he describes the test as follows:

> The test produces some four to twelve passages carefully selected from a literary work but presented in random sequence. It asks students to read and recollect these passages in order to restore their correct order. Unlike an essay examination, it does not ask them, in response to a pointed question, to render the book's 'meaning' in their own prose. Nor does it force students into the bifurcating logic of their instructor's interpretation as the multiple choice examination does. Neither does it call for short-answer identification of 'the facts' implied by each passage. It merely asks for the original sequence of the sample passages. That is all, because everything else is implied.

Clearly such a test will never replace essays and term papers, nor was it meant to. But whether used as (part of) an exam, or in the course of the semester's work, it is not only objective but also time-saving. As Huntley points out, such a test takes 15 minutes to make, 15 minutes to take, and 15 minutes to grade accurately (for an entire class). I have not yet dared to introduce it in Copenhagen. But some day I will.

Drama in the Classroom

Karl-Heinz Westarp, University of Aarhus, Denmark

Even before Stanley Fish's famous question 'Is There a Text in This Class?' (Fish 1980) problematized the existence of any given text as an entity separate from the reader, it was difficult enough to deal with literary texts as objects of analytical discourse: philological, stylistic, formalist, structuralist, deconstructionist and new-historicist models and methods tried to supply means for meaningful intersubjective communications about a series of black dots on blank pages. The translation process, i.e. lifting the black dots off the page, is an excruciatingly complex epistemological process, and the difficulties increase the further the actual experience is removed from the text's original time and language. This is difficult enough as far as poetry and fiction are concerned, but in the specific translation processes in relation to drama I consider the difficulties even greater, because studying a play as a literary text in the classroom is an 'amputated' or 'alienated' way of experiencing drama. As teachers of drama, then, we must be particularly concerned with preserving the unique cultural value of drama so aptly described by Joyce Carol Oates:

> Drama is our highest communal celebration of the mystery of being, and of the mystery of our being together, in relationships we struggle to define, and which define us. It makes the point, ceaselessly, that our lives are *now*; there is no history that is not *now*. (Oates 1991:1)

Tadeusz Kowzan has identified no less than thirteen sign systems simultaneously at work in dramatic performance, viz. 'words, voice inflection, facial mimicry, gesture, body movement, make-up, headdress, costume, accessory, stage design, lighting, music, and noise' (Eco 1990:115). On the basis of Kowzan's catalogue Umberto Eco defines drama as the one art form 'in which the whole of human experience is co-involved ... in which human bodies, artifacts, music, literary expressions (and therefore literature, painting, music, architecture and so on) are in play at the same moment' (115). How can one ever hope to decode all those sign systems in connection with a drama course in a literature department? Nevertheless, the rich tradition of drama cannot simply be cut from our curricula because of the inherent difficulty of teaching it as drama. The challenge must be taken up, and in the following I shall try to delineate my way of dealing with drama in class.

In order to throw the shortcomings of my own approach into perspective I should like to preface it with Umberto Eco and Martin Esslin's discussion of the late-nineteenth-century American philosopher Charles S. Peirce's example of semiotic 'ostension': 'A drunkard exposed in a public place by the Salvation Army in order to advertise the advantages of temperance' (Eco 1990:116). Eco convincingly analyses this example with all its signifying dimensions as the epitome of theatrical performance: 'A human body, along with its conventionally recognizable properties, surrounded by or supplied with a set of objects, inserted within a physical space, stands for something else to a reacting audience' (122). Esslin takes issue with Eco in pointing out that his use of Peirce's example is incomplete, since he did not point out the entire complexity of the actor's semiotic role. To Esslin the actor is also a 'real' person, who through empathy has transformed himself into a fictional character and ultimately in the spectator's mind becomes the 'fiction' itself: 'For the man here stands for a sign that stands for a man who, in turn, is recognised and valued as the original man that he is' (Esslin 1990:128). This 'personal' actor's dimension, neglected by Eco, is undoubtedly of paramount importance in the casting process as well as in the resultant impact of the performance. I agree with Esslin, but in my drama pedagogy I have so far left out the actor's 'personal' (or 'star') dimension.

In the various drama courses I have taught I have always made a point of getting the students into close contact with the actual performing process, either by discussing the text with its author or by sitting in on rehearsals and discussing details of the actual production with the director and some of the actors. We have also had directors and designers visit us in the classroom to familiarize us with their work in progress. It is extremely important for the understanding of a dramatic performance to see it grow, to see the end product – and then to compare expressed intentions with the actual result and with one's own understanding of the text. Though such arrangements are not always easy to make, particularly if, as in the case of English drama taught in an English department in Denmark, the actual performance takes place in a language and an environment different from the original. Yet the reward of bringing the play to life in this way has always turned out to be worth the effort.

The particular course I want to report on was an Open University course on 'Shakespeare and His Dramatic Compeers'. I was acutely aware of the difficulty of bridging the time gap, which in the case of drama seems to be even more striking than with non-dramatic literature, because changes in the conventions of acting, designing, lighting and playhouse architecture have to be taken into consideration as well. Though I could presuppose some level of theoretical awareness, I decided not to waste time on deconstructionist pursuits: we took the texts in their critically edited form as given facts from which to start.

After a couple of introductory lectures highlighting Elizabethan and Jacobean theatrical conventions and traditions, and foregrounding Marlowe, Shakespeare, Tourneur and Jonson against the general background of the period, the students were asked to read the first text. I gave them the clear instruction that they should not allow themselves to get bogged down in the details of notes and editorial cruxes: 'Read the text, get the gist of it and allow yourself to be captured by the characters, the dramatic conflict and its development. And do not refrain from sharing your gut reaction with us'.

Once these first impressions and reactions have been shared and discussed, the next phase is again restricted to the students' private study, and this is probably the most difficult and demanding exercise. Now the text and the characters must be studied in detail. In this process it is very important that the text be brought to life in the student's imagination: the student becomes the director who sets up his own subjective staging of the play, preferably with notes and small sketches.

What do the settings of each single scene look like, how do I handle the transition from one scene to the other? What do the characters look like, how are they to be blocked on the stage, how do they react to each other, how does their dialogue fit into the pattern of their movements? I consider this difficult translation process from the printed text to the vividly imagined staging of the play the single most essential step towards a thorough understanding: at this stage the students should be ready to stand back and see and write down the overall structures and themes in the play.

The next phase, which is based on the students' notes, takes place in class, where every single student should have a chance to present and argue for his/her production ideas and their link-up with an overall thematic and structural interpretation. After this round of presentation, the pros and cons of the suggested productions will be criticized and discussed in class. These discussions reveal with fascinating clarity the wide variety of readings possible of any given text. In order to enhance the understanding of the characters I assign parts to the students. In the following session they will enact those characters, using their own words and arguments, yet staying inside their original reading and understanding of the character. Not all students are ready to do this, yet it forces them to think more deeply about the characters and consider their possible relevance for a twentieth-century audience.

It is only after this intensive private study and extended in-class discussion about the play that I introduce the students to secondary texts. Now they are ready to judge other critics' premises and conclusions, since they can use their own interpretations and discussions as a valuable perspectivising backdrop. Unfortunately it happens much too often, I think, that students' interest in a play is deadened by a strictly academic approach. A play studied as a *literary* text only alienates it from its natural *dramatic* ambience, and if the students are asked to read secondary sources before having made up their minds about the play, they will be unduly prejudiced. If it is done the other way round, the study of other critics' opinions will help deepen and relativise the student's own interpretation of the play.

The actual experience of a production is the next important step in the process of teaching and understanding drama. In connection with the course on 'Shakespeare and His Dramatic Compeers' the students had, even before the course started, considered the possibility of arranging a theatre excursion to Stratford. Thus the choice of plays for the course was partly influenced by the programme for the Royal Shakespeare Company's season. Of the five productions we saw, three were plays that had been part of the course, viz. Marlowe's *The Jew of Malta*, Shakespeare's *The Merchant of Venice* and Tourneur's *The Revenger's Tragedy*. The week in Stratford was an intensive process of exposure to live drama. The play we were about to see later in the day was discussed in a two-hour session, partly to recapitulate major data about it or – in the case of the two plays that hadn't been studied before – to give brief introductions. All productions showed high standards of acting, design and directing, and they were all very different in style. After each performance we had another seminar session, in which we tried to get to grips with the special qualities of the production, its pros and cons. Another important issue was an attempt to compare the actual production with the one each of us had built up in our imagination and discussed in earlier sessions. Unfortunately we were unable to make arrangements with actors and/or directors of the plays to come and discuss their work with us. This would certainly have further enhanced the experience. In our discussions we touched upon the handling of almost all of Kowzan's sign systems. And as the days went by the level of awareness in relation to even the smallest details in the different sign systems increased.

Thanks to the fact that we saw both Marlowe's and Shakespeare's handling of the theme of the Jew, we were able start comparative analyses, in which parallels and differences in their respective treatment of language, character, setting and plot could be pointed out. This comparative approach was taken up again in the last session of the course in connection with these and the other playwrights presented in the course.

After the Stratford experience it was probably a badly planned anticlimax when I asked the students to work on the production of short scenes of their own choice and perform them in front of their fellow students. I did this partly because I wanted them to get a feel for the difficult job of performing but also to let them try to translate their academic knowledge of the entire play into the speaking of a few concrete lines from it. They performed to the best of their abilities, and I still think it was rewarding – and not only for the hilarious laughter it provoked at times.

To conclude: I think that it is only through a combination of the detailed study of the text and the various aspects of its transition to a proper theatrical *mise-en-scène* that drama, as a unique genre and mode of human communication, can survive in the classroom.

Teaching the Easy Text: A Practical-Theoretical Discussion of a Didactic Problem

Lars Ole Sauerberg, University of Odense, Denmark

I

Although we are on slippery ground when it comes to the distinction between literature and non-literature, and although ultimately it makes no sense to talk about hard and easy literary texts, since each text must be considered uniquely equal to its purpose, practical conditions in the classroom or the lecture hall remain virtually unaffected by such sophistry. School, college or university syllabi in English and American literature are almost invariably selections of undisputedly literary works based on accessibility within a generally accepted representational range: extremely easy as well as extremely hard texts are avoided, and the moderately-challenging-but-still-accessible text holds sway in the average reading list. In what follows I shall address myself to the problem of relative difficulty of accessibility in literary texts and suggest some possible principles of a rationale for dealing with the easy literary text.

II

The distinction between the easy and the hard literary text is a distinction arising in the didactic context, and the premises for the distinction consequently have to do with teaching circumstances rather than with aesthetics.

Some literary texts are considered hard to teach mainly for one of two reasons: either they are felt to be highly complex, or they are felt to be overlong for often quite limited course dimensions.

Textual complexity may be in the nature of either structural or semantic obstacles, or of both in interaction. (Indeed, semantics may be seen as a structural problem, but this has no relevance for the present discussion.) Structural and semantic complexity arises when the literary text deviates from accepted patterns; this applies to the literary text both in relation to non-literary texts and in relation to other literary texts.

Most readers find themselves at home with a prose-fiction text – a short story or a novel – in the realistic tradition. Its narrative structure is felt to be natural, although the familiar plot allowing for all loose ends to be tied up authoritatively is, of course, a violation by simplification of the multi-patterned reality which the text supposedly reflects. But a whole civilization's reliance on a beginning-middle-and-end plot matrix has made us reluctant to assimilate alternative structurations. Even when, as in the case of many modernist writers of narrative fiction, an approach is made to accommodate chaotic reality and to foreground a consistently limited point of view, this is felt by many readers as a move away from the natural into the contrived. The development of Virginia Woolf's narrative structure from traditional realism in *The Voyage Out* (1915) to modernist experimentation with point of view and plot in *The Waves* (1931) is a good illustration of how a change intended to bring the literary text closer to reality has scared readers away. Although this writer's narrative development is a strictly logical radicalization of narrative technique, most readers probably feel that her novels become harder and harder to read, taken in their chronological sequence. The work of many metafictional writers, who deliberately call into doubt the validity of acknowledged structures as well as of perceiving consciousnesses, will also give the reader difficulties. Finally, to draw on the present author's experience from a university-extension course on contemporary British literature, it requires quite an effort to bring an audience of fairly well-educated but elderly readers brought up on mainstream realism into sympathetic alignment with the multiple endings of John Fowles's *The French Lieutenant's Woman* (1969) or with the convolutions of D. M. Thomas's five volumes of daring improvisation collectively titled *Russian Nights* (1983-90).

Semantic complexity, understood as a deviation from conventional verbal combinations, is often considered *the* characteristic of poetic texts, with their tradition for metaphor-saturated language condensed and twisted beyond comprehensibility. It does not take much reading of Ezra Pound or Geoffrey Hill to reach the point of semantic desperation. The cause for despair in reading Pound or Hill is, however, of a kind allowed for by the rules of language for poetry. In the novel too, though certainly less often than in poetry, we may find semantic complexity 'obscuring' the content of the narrative. When the language becomes too 'poetic,' the text may be felt to be at cross purposes with its truly denotative self, as in the case of James Joyce's *Finnegans Wake* (1939) with its famous/notorious disfigurations of familiar words and phrases.

The case of *Finnegans Wake* invites us to consider the additional problem of difficulty of accessibility created by intertextuality. When we talk about structural familiarity, we assume knowledge of a number of texts of the same kind, to which the experience of reading each new one can be related. And in the area of semantics we assume familiarity with words and phrases, and the way that we usually combine them. But echoes may be heard in a text from other texts, echoes sometimes clear, sometimes distorted to the point of unrecognizability. No doubt texts which signal clearly the need for above-average literary experience, as do many texts by, for example, Eliot, Stevens, Pound, and Hill, scare many, even fairly well-educated, readers away.

The other kind of hard text regularly avoided for teaching purposes is the very long text, which need not, however, be structurally or semantically complicated, just long. A basic reason for the massive success of New Criticism was the happy mixture of the underlying ideological assumption of textual autonomy (no context required) with analytical focus on the 'elementary particles' of the text requiring only brief – and, preferably, signally self-contained – passages of text. (For most practical classroom use the formalist aspect of New Criticism rather than its dogmatic leaning on irony, paradox, ambiguity, etc. must be assumed to have received emphasis.) New Criticism never really reconciled itself with texts longer than could be taken in by a single sweep of the eye, with the result that next to no useful criticism of narrative fiction or epic poetry was produced during the golden era of that critical approach. Even today, with practical criticism still having a firm foundation in New Criticism and Formalism, teachers feel they have the tools for work on relatively short and metaphor-saturated texts, but lack the critical apparatus for work on the novel, the epic, and even the short story. Add to that the obvious practical difficulties involved in portioning out the long text in the classroom or lecture hall. Are long texts like Byron's *Don Juan* (1819-24) or *Childe Harold* (1809-18) to be divided up into sections convenient for a session's discussion, forcing the analyst to rely on a principle of progression in his analysis, with the inevitable result that summary must take up much of the time in order to ensure coherence? Or can the whole text be counted on as read and taken in by the students, in order for the analyst to range freely from A to Z? Even if the latter possibility is perhaps preferable in principle, it will be realistic to assume that the text has been read *in toto* by only a limited number in the audience, and perhaps not fully digested even by them.

To deal analytically with the long text in class often means paraphrase with heavy support from general commentary, or parcelling out in extracts, or using the text as a historical document to highlight general or specific text-contemporary issues. Sustained and consistent analysis of book-length texts is not for the classroom, and only seldom for the lecture hall. It belongs by its nature to written criticism, and hence syllabi seldom contain the whole text of epics like Spenser's *The Faerie Queene* (1596), Milton's *Paradise Lost* (1667), Byron's *Don Juan* (1819-24), or long novels or novel sequences like the Victorian three-volume novel or a modern *roman fleuve* like Anthony Powell's *A Dance to the Music of Time* (1951-75), not to speak of texts like Joyce's *Ulysses*

(1922) and *Finnegans Wake* or Thomas Pynchon's *Gravity's Rainbow* (1973), which qualify simultaneously for both categories of didactic difficulty by virtue of structural/semantic complication *and* length.

III

The moderately challenging text preferred for teaching purposes is the kind of text which, in a quantitative perspective, is short enough to be dealt with in a satisfactory manner in one or two sessions, and, in a qualitative perspective, complicated enough to give the analyst sufficient matter to explicate the strength of the text itself. But explication, that is the correlation of all elements in a text to each other so that a consistent reading is the result, is often taken to be synonymous with the decoding or the disentanglement of the text, on the analogy of solving a puzzle. The typical text singled out for critical attention is the kind of text which requires some kind of key, possessed by the teacher, to be handed over triumphantly in class.

Examples of the teachable text will dominate in most syllabi, and a few texts from my current reading list for my course in practical criticism will no doubt receive nods of recognition: Kate Chopin's 'Two Portraits' (1895), Jon Stallworthy's 'The Almond Tree' (1969), Sherwood Anderson's 'Paper Pills' (from *Winesburg, Ohio*, 1919), Doris Lessing's 'Wine' (1957), T. S. Eliot's 'The Love Song of J. Alfred Prufrock' (1915), and Ted Hughes's 'River' (1983). These are all texts which pose no extreme verbal problems, but which are certain to raise problems of a kind which only a helping hand from the teacher can solve. The short story by Sherwood Anderson, to pick one example, is felt to be as awkward as literary text as the doctor it features until the structural resemblance to the paper pills of the title, supported by the twisted-apple imagery, suddenly reveals it as a text with a deliberately crooked structure. Doris Lessing's short story, to pick another example, makes its point by subtle nuance and innuendo, which requires careful analysis of the psychological situation in combination with an appreciation of imagery and structure to lay bare. This is plainly work for the counselling teacher. And so on and so forth. The teachable text obviously requires exegesis, and thus institutional efforts are justified.

IV

Easy texts are easy in that they pose no immediate problems for the reader's understanding in the sense of contextualization in terms of the familiar. Most of them are considered to stand in a simple metonymical relationship with the experiential world as communicated verbally for other than literary purposes, which is, however, a problematical critical position (see below). Examples are legion, but a few taken from the last four hundred years of English and American literary history will give an indication of the kind of text under consideration: Ben Jonson's 'To Penshurst' (1616), Wordsworth's 'We Are Seven' (1798), Browning's 'Home-Thoughts, from Abroad' (1845), Hemingway's short stories, Larkin's 'Ambulances' (1964), Andrew Motion's 'Anne Frank Huis' (1983). All these texts have in common their unproblematic accessibility, with no apparent need for sophisticated scholarly apparatus. Although all of them are comparatively short and therefore, in principle, quantitatively suited for classroom purposes, none of them have that just-above-student-ability puzzle characteristic, which in combination with brief length seems to make for optimal teachability.

Because of their immediate accessibility such texts pose an obvious problem for the teacher, who sees his function as qualified/qualifying mediator reduced considerably. But of course it is not only a question of didactic power politics. Many teachers feel lost facing easy texts, as their analytical equipment has been developed for far more sophisticated problems. If texts like these are, after all, included in syllabi, their lack of qualitative challenge will often be compensated for by added quantity: instead of one Larkin poem we will supply a list of five!

The teacher forced to teach the easy text will often resort to steeping the text in text-external commentary. The tendency in such cases is for information about cultural, political, economic, etc. contexts to be especially plentiful. To return to the examples above: Ben Jonson's neat and idyllic 'To Penshurst' will be read as a text typical of Neoclassicism, with careful pointing out of classical models and allusions; Wordsworth's contrivedly simple 'We Are Seven' will be related to his and Coleridge's 'Preface' programme as a manifestation of the ideals set up there; Browning's nostalgic 'Home-Thoughts, from Abroad' will give occasion to talk about the poet's personal circumstances and the condition of Victorian England; Hemingway's short stories will lead into a discussion of heroic codes, very likely with excursions into myth; Larkin's kitchen-sink-style 'Ambulances' invites comment as an example of post-World-War-Two disillusioned realism; and Andrew Motion's near-sentimental 'Anne Frank Huis' of course requires filling in of Holocaust background. However, in all these cases we feel that by providing contexts we are removing ourselves centrifugally from their characteristics as *literary* texts rather than staying in close contact. Contextual commentary is of course fully legitimate as a critical approach, but the classroom and survey-course situations hardly provide the best conditions for pursuing that line of study to the point of critical satisfaction.

V

But how do we, as teachers of all literature, not just the not-particularly-easy-nor-particularly-hard texts, handle the easy ones in a way which makes us feel that we are not cheating by dodging the issue?

A first step would be to recognize that in easy as well as in in-between and hard texts we are dealing with the same kind of text-discourse function, which is a function different from the kinds of discourse we use for other – non-literary – purposes. In other words, that texts with a literary function require a kind of attention qualitatively different from the one we give to other modes of verbal communication.

Instead of abandoning the easy text at once in order to situate it historically, socially, etc., we should start by zooming in on the traits in the text which invite the reader to readjust his expectations in accordance with the literary function. Such an approach is an inversion of Northrop Frye's recommendation, in *Anatomy of Criticism* (1957), to stand further and further back from the detail in order eventually to arrive at a kind of totality, with, as he insists in that work, truly liberating effects for the reader.

Starting with the postulate that the literary function is a question of an imaginative order alternative to experiential reality, which provides a *deliberately evaluating perspective*, I shall sketch a scenario for analysis which is equally applicable to all texts, but all the more called-for in the case of the easy text, because this is so often approached on premises of dubious critical purpose. I shall do so by calling attention to ideas and principles to do with epistemology and aesthetics, which may not be the latest fashion in Theory but which are nonetheless useful for the matter in hand. I do not claim any startling new insights, but hope merely to call attention to a basic critical awareness which often vanishes from sight in the case of the difficult or the teachable text, and therefore is not readily in mind when dealing with the easy text.

VI

In his celebrated 'Closing Statement: Linguistics and Poetics' (in Sebeok 1960), Roman Jakobson introduced a communication model which has proved its usefulness both to the strategies of hard-core structuralists who dominated the critical field from about that time until the late 70s and to the more modest goals of everyday critical pedagogy.

In brief, the model was designed to show that various kinds of textual function may be attributed to various positions in the communication situation, with the 'poetic function' being the complement of the 'fundamental factor' of the 'message.' The poetic function, according to Jakobson, *'projects the principle of equivalence from the axis of selection into the axis of combination'* (Sebeok 1960:358; Jakobson's italics). In his paper Jakobson is obviously concerned with poetry in the narrow sense of the term, as he proceeds to illustrate, using examples from prosody. Still, his suggested principle holds good for the poetic, understood as the literary, function of language in general, as argued by David Lodge in *The Modes of Modern Writing: Metaphor, Metonymy, and the Typology of Modern Literature* (1977).

Lodge's modification of Jakobson's exclusive concentration on verbal elements as constituting the poetic function includes recommendations by Fish and Todorov to rely on a wholly pragmatic and reader-related concept of literature. Referring to H. G. Widdowson's distinction between text and discourse – the 'linguistic form of a literary work and the function of its language in the communication of meaning' respectively (Lodge 1977:6) – Lodge proposes 'fictionality' as the characteristic deviance of the literary discourse. Lodge's idea of fictionality rests somewhat loosely on J. L. Austin's distinction between constative and performative utterances (see Austin 1962): 'It would seem that we can identify literature with fiction only in the weak, negative sense that in the literary text, descriptions and propositions *need* not be put forward or accepted as "true"' (2). He suggests in consequence that 'literary discourse is either self-evidently fictional or may be read as such, and that what compels or permits such reading is the structural organization of its component parts, its systematic foregrounding' (6-7). What we read as literary texts may be felt as such because they are either 'axiomatically' literary, that is, because there is 'no other recognized category of discourse of which they could be instances [or] if enough readers like them for "literary" reasons' (7). In spite of the invitation by these observations to make the 'literary' a question of receptional processing, Lodge insists that literary reading presupposes familiarity with axiomatically literary texts, since 'writing requires reading for its completion, but also teaches the kind of reading it requires' (9). Lodge's discussion of the readerly/functional as opposed to the structural/textual definition of literature allows him to arrive at a definition of literature as an 'open category', which may contain all kinds of discourse read as literature, 'but only on condition that such discourse has something in common with the discourse that you cannot take out of it: the something being a structure which either indicates the fictionality of a text or enables a text to be read as if it were fictional' (9). In more pragmatic terms, a text, then, is literary either if it is already accepted as such, or if the reader wants to read it as literature and is able to justify this approach by pointing to 'fictional' elements in the text.

According to Jakobson, poetic function is a question of projecting the principle of equivalence from the axis of selection into the axis of combination, and according to Lodge the literary is a question of fictionality, that is, a conventional codification of the text into a literary discourse on the proposition that it is not necessarily true. The decision to read a text as literary or non-literary in most cases poses no problem: a computer manual will hardly be an object of literary appreciation. The function of the text is determined by its intended function, and the intention is clear from a variety of textual signals. And *vice versa:* the text chosen for non-useful purposes will typically be the literary text, but of course texts which are not clearly signalled as literary may also be read as if they were literature in the narrow sense of the term. If this is so, it must be possible to see in such texts elements known from axiomatically literary texts or from other texts already related to axiomatically literary texts. That a text may shift its function in this respect is a familiar phenomenon: a historian reading a biography to support his research does not read it as Mr. General Reader, who reads it 'merely' for entertainment.

Once it has been decided to read the text as literary, which in itself is hardly a fully actualized process of thought, the reader shifts his priorities in terms of combination and selection. But the reason why such a shift is at all possible is that the literary text does not relate directly to reality, but, as argued by Richard Ohmann in his discussion of Austin on speech acts, '*imitates* a standard discourse' (Ohmann 1971:16), producing what I have chosen to term a second-order illocutionary act in contrast to what may be termed a first-order illocutionary act 'with standard referential intent'. Second-order speech acts relate to an always implicit or potential counter-text in the literary text. In other words, I suggest, the literary text must be thought of as playing against the potential non-literary text, combining the discourse elements of that non-existing text in such a way that it reveals a deliberately evaluating perspective, which is not, or is only incidentally, the case of its non-literary counter-text. (To remain in Austin's terminology, for a first-order discourse to foreground a literary function would be infelicitous.) For that purpose the literary text draws on time-proven effects of the axiomatically literary. Critical analysis is able to make explicit the properties in the text that can be seen as the meeting point of such an evaluating perspective on an existential situation and the aesthetic – combinative – tools by which it is made unique and literary.

In practice, this dynamic of second-order illocution expressive of a set of values in terms of the axiomatically literary is to be appreciated first and foremost for its implicit and explicit contrasts to the characteristics of the – potential – non-literary text, that is for its evaluating perspective and the conventional means by which it is achieved. Consequently, the reading of any literary text must begin as an overall appreciation of its literary 'otherness' which is really its 'selfness'. This applies to all texts read as literature, but foregroundedly complex and/or long texts will of course most readily signal their otherness. However, the easy text displays its literary otherness as well.

Although the literary otherness in most texts read as literature is a matter of recognizing axiomatically literary elements such as verse and chapter divisions or rhyme and rhythm, these are elements, in the present perspective, which do not by themselves constitute the literary in a text, but serve as historically determined markers of the second-order illocutionary discourse. This is not to suggest that they are contingent. On the contrary, they are the means by which literary otherness is achieved, the appreciation of which, to make a long story short, is a matter of laying bare its difference from its 'Siamese twin', the implied illocutionary counter-text(s). On that basis I suggest that a central concern for critical analysis should always be the reading of the text in terms of the combination of structures which makes it a deliberate evaluation of existence as communicated in implicit or potential first-order illocutionary counter-texts.

It is a premise of my argument that central to a literary text is its deliberate evaluation of a potential first-order text. Inevitably 'deliberate' because the creative mind, in shifting the equivalence principle, that is, in devising a form, produces an alternative signification which, as mere difference or contrast, is an act of evaluation by virtue of re-ordering. It may be objected that not all literary texts display such a deliberate evaluation of what they are about. And, conversely, that texts, like the political speech, the sermon, the speeches of counsel in court, etc., make a point of deliberate evaluation. However, the difference between a sermon, etc. and literature is that the evaluating bias of these first-order speech acts has a quite definite aim: to change the situation referred to in them. This is not the case with the second-order discourse of literature, at any rate only when it becomes the first-order texts of didactic literature. All literary texts are evaluations, but in relation to potential first-order texts, with no *immediate* bearing on reality. The evaluation central in the literary text, like Wallace Stevens's famous jar in Tennessee, has no specific use value.

To argue my point in some practical-analytical detail, I have chosen an easy text by a contemporary poet, Andrew Motion's 'Anne Frank Huis' (Motion 1984:41).

VII

ANNE FRANK HUIS

Even now, after twice her lifetime of grief
and anger in the very place, whoever comes
to climb these narrow stairs, discovers how
the bookcase slides aside, then walks through
shadow into sunlit rooms, can never help

but break her secrecy again. Just listening
is a kind of guilt: the Westerkirk repeats

itself outside, as if all time worked round
towards her fear, and made each stroke
die down on guarded streets. Imagine it –

three years of whispering and loneliness
and plotting, day by day, the Allied line
in Europe with a yellow chalk. What hope
she had for ordinary love and interest
survives her here, displayed above the bed

as pictures of her family; some actors;
fashions chosen by Princess Elizabeth.
And those who stoop to see them find
not only patience missing its reward,
but one enduring wish for chances

like my own: to leave as simply
as I do, and walk at ease
up dusty tree-lined avenues, or watch
a silent barge come clear of bridges
settling their reflections in the blue canal.

This is the kind of poem that teachers of literature either shy away from because
there seems to be no critical challenge in it, that is, no secret doors to prise
open, or which they try to provide with a literature-external background by
setting off at a tangent about the Holocaust. Of course, the appreciation of the
poem requires a general background to the events of World War Two. This is
part of the semantic field of the text, as is some general knowledge about
Amsterdam required to evoke the right mood of the setting. But it is possible to
make these semantic fields part of an appreciation pivoted on the text as
literature, not just a neat versification of history and geography.

Motion's poem is a combination of words, phrases, sounds, and rhythms
serving to communicate a specific attitude, a deliberately evaluating perspective,
to events from the past, so as to achieve a certain existential angle, an ordering
of chaos. In contrast to reality, that is, history and geography on the one hand
and the poet's life on the other, the poem is, by definition as literature, a
microcosm, a unity. The equivalence principle is at work in the text fundamentally as the bringing together, in a unified vision, these disparate historical and
personal strands with an individual consciousness, in order to create an
evaluating second-order illocutionary discourse. The literary otherness or
peculiarity of the text lies in its combination of such strands under the
assumption of equivalence within this second-order discourse. So an introductory
analytical step would be to determine the angle of the persona's imaginative
vision and its consequences for the subject matter of the poem. This is,
admittedly, a routine in critical analysis. However, its central importance is often

overlooked, especially in the case of the easy text, because the angle of vision is felt to be a matter of uncomplicated naturalization, to use Jonathan Culler's term (Culler 1975), with the implication that it craves no special attention. (A parallel situation is to be found in the way that misunderstandings may often occur as a result of a reader's assumption of familiarity with a word which would have turned out to have another meaning had he thought to look it up.) In Motion's poem, the reader might be tempted to pass over the angle of vision, because it presents itself 'naturally' as a tourist's reflections on a recent visit to Anne Frank's house. Nothing strange in that. However, when the equivalence principle is shifted from selection to combination, the event is no longer the situation beside the canal in Amsterdam, but the text as situation. The angle of vision, in the house as well as outside, is clearly dominated by a sense of guilt. The feeling of guilt is the basis of equivalence for the whole experience and makes the relation of events – past and present – into the uniqueness of the poem as second-order discourse. The feeling of guilt is expressed plainly in stanza two, but can be seen to saturate the text from beginning to end: the unease about violating something private in stanza one, the gloomy evocation of the past by the Westerkirk bells in stanza two, the almost forced empathy in stanza three, the near-sentimentality produced by the observation of trivia in stanza four, and the feeling of cheapness by the undeserved relief in stanza five.

Complementary to the angle of vision unified by the feeling of guilty conscience is a kind of versification which in itself is a sophistication of the equivalence principle which Jakobson sees as an inherent characteristic of verse. Motion's poem is in blank verse, but it is very irregular blank verse, broken up into verse paragraphs whose regular line count makes them qualify as stanzas, with a variable number of feet and a highly irregular rhythm. Add to that the characteristic of run-on lines, within stanzas and from stanza to stanza. In other words, the text, under the aspect of versification, constantly defies the striving towards rhythmical equivalence characteristic of verse. But the defiance is so dominant as to constitute another kind of equivalence, and the experience of this recurring flight away from the regularity which is ingrained in the reader by his past experience of the axiomatically literary, leaves the reader with a feeling of a persona reacting by hesitation against the foreseeable and trying to find his bearings in a situation of obvious confusion. The blank spaces between stanzas one and two, three and four, and four and five, separating a coherent syntax, enhance the effect of hesitation before finding the proper continuation. Especially fraught is the situation described in the transition from stanzas four to five, where the specification of chances not available to Anne Frank, as to the persona himself, makes the effect of the verse pattern coincide with the guilt angle of vision.

The analysis sketched out above has as its tacit counter-text a first-order illocutionary potential, which would consist of a number of speech acts or discourses. They would include, roughly, the history 'text' of the Frank family, that is the published diary of Anne, the history 'text' of the Nazi persecution of Jews during World War Two, the geography 'text' of Amsterdam, and the psychology 'text' of the poet. All these may be constituted as first-order illocutionary discourses, as independent non-literary texts. And as such they may of course express attitudes and biases, indeed can hardly help but do so. But that, at any rate, is not their main purpose. In the literary text, the poem, these separate texts merge into a textual form under a deliberately evaluating perspective shaped by the shift from the verbal conventions of first-order acts to the meta-level of second-order acts. The literary text makes the most of this ambiguity by which words refer to both reality and other words. In the poem the various reality texts are subsumed in a different reality, which is purely verbal. The rules of poetry exploit the ambiguity between the two levels in the way that verbal constellations typical of first-order acts are broken up and re-combined in the second-order constructions to create a new verbal reality. This 'reality' is wholly of the second order, according to Jakobson's equivalence principle, but is readily 'misunderstood' as first order. It actually exploits the possibility of that misunderstanding.

An analysis in terms of a deliberately evaluating perspective does not avoid the danger lurking in all analyses setting out from a high level of abstraction: how to prove its adequacy and exactitude. There is no other way than to test it against the pertinent elements in the text, which is really what the analysis is all about. Still, the discussion about the validity of competing hypotheses about evaluating perspectives is in itself of central interest to the text under scrutiny, because the testing ground will necessarily be elements in the text, not extraneous matter.

VIII

The principles of the tentative analysis of Andrew Motion's 'Anne Frank Huis' apply to all literary texts, but are especially pertinent in the case of the easy text. The analysis outlined above accepts the text as a response to existence unified as a second-order illocutionary discourse in a given perspective, which is inevitably an evaluation of impressions from what can be rendered in first-order illocutionary discourses. Such an approach does not treat the text as a riddle, but attempts to find the unifying element in the particular combination of elements which makes the text into something other in relation to reality as expressed in a potential first-order illocutionary act. Nor do the principles reduce the text to the favoured ambiguity of New Criticism, to the simulacrum of Structuralism, to the evasiveness of Deconstruction. There is no need, either, for recourse to the huge contexts needed by historical criticism, ranging from traditional biography to Neo-Marxism and New Historicism. The principles are applied in an attempt to do justice to the poem as something unique but generally accessible and, important for criticism, worth the effort of analytical work without the critic feeling that he is getting into tautological paraphrase, or reading into the text unnecessary convolutions and complications, or setting off at a tangent away from the text into the infinite space of commentary. A literary text, easy or hard, deserves attention as the particular species of verbal discourse it is and for the particular existential function it serves.

You Can Take It with You: Reading to Live

Marianne Thormählen, University of Lund, Sweden

One of Flaubert's letters exhorts the recipient not to read for amusement, the way children do, nor like the ambitious for instruction, but read *pour vivre* (Flaubert 1903:329-30). It is not one of those dicta that immediately reduce one to awed silence; for one thing, most people would probably agree that amusement and instruction are fairly important aspects of life. For all its oracularity, though, it makes a claim for reading which I find difficult to disregard. Ours is not an age of lofty ideals, and anyone who articulates exalted ambitions in the field of literary teaching must expect to encounter varying degrees of derision from more or less jaded colleagues. Even so, I would not be satisfied watching my students leave the room after a literary seminar if I did not feel confident that they would take the text we had been working on with them, and keep it with them for at least part of their lives.

1. Principles

Like any other university teacher of English literature, I want my students to master the basics of our academic discipline, from metrical feet to metaphors and Metaphysical poets. Students just under, at, or over the graduate level are also entitled to expect that the tuition they receive should include information about the various approaches to literary texts that have featured in the development of the discipline. That includes contemporary directions in literary criticism and scholarship. If students are going on to, or are already involved in, doing research, they will need such orientation in order to establish a basis for their own contributions. Grasping the principal lines of thought and argumentation put forward by predecessors and contemporaries will sharpen the students' awareness of textual dimensions, irrespective of whether they agree with, reject, or feel doubtful about the views and stances articulated by various 'established' authors.

Still, I have always felt – though I am aware that many of my colleagues would challenge that feeling – that the test of any literary method comes when it is applied to the actual study of a text. The decisive question, to me, is: Does the application of a particular perspective show me anything in the text that I did not see before, thereby enriching my appreciation of it? Hence, my attempts to make students familiar with various theoretical approaches are always directly associated with the reading of a literary work. At this moment, courses in 'theory' are taught at English departments all over the world. Valuable as I am sure they often are, the shortage of hours available for literary tuition at Swedish universities makes it seem more expedient to prove the puddings in the eating, fitting theory into seminars on literature rather than devoting seminars to theory alone.

The literary text, then, is where all academic effort begins and ends. Consequently, my chief aim has always been that of helping a text come alive in the minds of new readers, and all the components that make up my idea of a good literary seminar are rooted in the ambition to bring students and texts together. Those components will be reviewed in the following pages, but one issue raised by this book's editor should be addressed first. It ties up with my introductory reflections on the quotation from Flaubert: What is the use of reading books? Is that pursuit 'a somewhat anachronistic exercise' in the Nineties, given the range and far-reaching effects of the media, etc.?

The idea that close association with literature is somehow ennobling is one I do not think many people would maintain. The prevalence of unappealing personalities among great writers dispels the notion, as does the lack of integrity and rectitude shown by too many academics in our field. Reading does not make us better; but it offers insights into various facets of the human predicament we all share – insights which we may, if our personal qualities allow it, turn to good uses. Quite apart from the utilitarian aspect, reading provides aesthetic pleasure, intellectual satisfaction, and emotional stimulation – in its happiest moments, all of these at the same time.

Those claims can also be made for a gripping television serial, though. What sets literature apart from such cultural phenomena is that it is made of words and words only. The reader absorbs them, lets his/her imagination and experience work on them (perhaps dropping some and manhandling others), and they become his/her mental property. As such, they are independent of the representational efforts of others and of such material considerations as the delivery of electric current. Put on paper, they can go anywhere and at any time. Learnt by heart – according to the pedagogical method that was the mainstay of education for thousands of years and has now, sadly, all but vanished – they live in our minds without requiring any tangible material at all. We can take them with us, for they belong to us. We clothe our sorrows in them, gaining comfort from the recognition that someone was there before us. Hanging on to the words that person left as a record, we may find the strength to move on, as he or she did. We use them to express and enhance our joys and commitments; and the scenes, characters, etc. created by writers of drama and fiction form a reservoir of experience – however indirect – that may help us grasp and cope with conditions affecting our own lives. All the time, the words of literary texts give us the reassurance – rare in our secular age – that comes from being part of a context larger than ourselves, whether or not we are clearly aware of it.

As if playing a part in the transmission of such precious stuff were not enough, we who teach literature have an awesome collective function: that of modifying the 'canon' of texts passed on to a new generation. Every one of us has a part to play in that process, however puny our individual stature in the total scheme of things. That conviction has influenced my choice of texts for teaching from the first. Pessimism induced by the progressive reduction of classic set texts in the teaching of English literature in my own country has made me a staunch 'mainstreamer' and led to a determined concentration on pre-1960 works. Many lists of set books for students of English at English departments in Sweden consist virtually exclusively of contemporary fiction. Meeting the leading authors of one's own time through the skilful mediation of an enthusiastic and knowledgeable academic teacher can be a great experience, and students are surely entitled to it. By and large, though, I feel no personal obligation to take part in such activities; so many colleagues are already doing it so well. Instead, I remain quixotically dedicated to the older masters and mistresses, and I think the kind of assistance I am able to offer students will be more useful to them when they tackle Pope and Yeats than when they approach Brookner and Atwood.

The emphasis on contemporary texts, particularly novels, which I have frequently found in present-day literary tuition has fostered the development of a somewhat heretical stance on my part: opposition against the pedagogical dogma (predominant in Sweden for decades) that students find it easier to 'relate to' works 'closely connected with their own situation or environment'. That contention seems to me to discount the imaginative powers and needs of young people (I do not think it is true of children either) in a downright insulting manner. Practical experience backs me up: Two seminars which were still in progress when the night watchman came round with his Alsatian had ended by bringing up the prospects of a) Caliban after Prospero's departure; b) the second Knightley-Woodhouse marriage. It would be hard, I think, to imagine two settings farther removed from the students' own everyday environment than Prospero's island and Austen's rural upper-class communities. Even so, a group of students spent hours after a class hotly debating the possible *future* fortunes of those figments of authorial imagination. It is a heartening memory.

2. Practice

Rather than selecting one text to serve as a basis for a 'pedagogical scenario', I have preferred to pick illustrations from seminars taught over a period of ten years. The reason why such a piecemeal approach seemed permissible is that my objectives when teaching seminars do not vary a great deal. Hence, the basic practical outline tends to be the same, whether seminars deal with Dryden or Auden.

2.1 The introductory mini-lecture

Starting each seminar by presenting an outline of the historical and cultural circumstances in which a literary work was created is usually essential. In addition, a biographical sketch of the author is helpful when it comes to stimulating student interest. This focus on authorial identity goes right against much present-day theory; but strange though it may sound, I have often found that such introductions are greatly appreciated. Normally, I have tried to obtain the most recent scholarly biography of the writer concerned, supplementing it with previous works whenever that seemed desirable.

In putting the biographical sketches together, I have no compunction about including popularising material, as long as I feel reasonably confident that it has a basis in fact. Anecdotes, juicy gossip, and funny or moving passages from letters are all grist to the mill. Often these 'tabloid items' remain when all else is forgotten, and why begrudge students a whiff of humour or pathos? Besides, the pedagogue who said that a class where the students had not laughed once was a bad class surely had a point.

This kind of material is not usually found in handbooks. Nor is another element which I try to include in my talks on authors: a conscious attempt to create a favourable 'climate of opinion' among students, increasing their willingness to give the author's work an interested hearing. Edwin Muir, a famous teacher as well as a fine poet, critic, and translator, is a source of inspiration in this respect. At a time when other literary authorities pontificated, or attacked other writers for adopting outmoded or traitorous attitudes, Muir took pains to be fair at all times and sympathetic whenever possible (Butter 1962:37-38). This does not, of course, amount to an advocacy of blandness, or of repressing student antipathy.

2.2 Student participation and 'study questions'

As everybody who has taught Swedish students knows, anarchy due to students 'taking over' during seminar discussions is a rare state of things indeed. The opposite problem is all too familiar: persuading students to participate freely in a relaxed discussion can be uphill work. If there is such a thing as a Swedish national character, terror of making oneself conspicuous has to be a main ingredient. In a way, the few who are unaffected by it suffer, too; spontaneously communicative students have been known to apologise for 'talking too much'. It is not always easy to convince them that they are the ones who have got it right. Incidentally, oral proficiency in English seems to matter less than personal characteristics; some of my most talkative students have actually spoken English rather badly, but refused to let that fact silence them.

Faced with the possibility of embarrassed, and embarrassing, silences, only one course seemed open to me: that of submitting guidelines for discussion in advance, in the form of 'study questions'. Encouraging active student participation by affording an opportunity to prepare answers is not the only rationale behind these questions, though. Some of them are set up in order to provide a basis for protracted and diligent homework, and it would not be fair to spring them on even the most uninhibited audience. By and large, I have found six types of study questions helpful. The ensuing paragraphs offer examples of these categories, referring to literature from the early eighteenth to the late nineteenth century.

1. Close-reading exercises. Questions of this kind can only be answered by people who have read the text in its entirety, with great concentration and attention to detail. Examples:

> a) William Morris, 'The Defence of Guenevere'. 'All I have said is truth, by Christ's dear tears'. Quite a commodity to swear by – do you think Guenevere speaks the truth? What exactly does her 'defence' amount to? Study her speech carefully, noting just what she admits and what she denies.
> b) Matthew Arnold, 'Stanzas from the Grande Chartreuse'. The shifting pronouns in this poem have contributed to its seeming complexity. Try to identify who 'we', 'thou', 'you', and 'they' are throughout the poem.

2. Matters of craftsmanship. These questions address such things as prosody, style (including rhetorical figures, alliteration, etc.), narratological aspects, and so forth. Examples:

> a) P.B. Shelley, 'Adonais'. Shelley had used the Spenserian stanza in his long poem *The Revolt of Islam* (12 cantos, albeit fairly short ones), so had had plenty of experience with this difficult metre when choosing it for 'Adonais'. Even his detractors admire the music

of the stanza in this poem. As an approach to the reasons for its excellence, analyse the effects employed by Shelley in stanzas xxxix and xl.

b) Robert Browning, 'Fra Lippo Lippi'. Lippo's language serves to characterise him. Look at the stylistic features, observing the range between vulgarisms and faithful reproductions of clerical usage. Also, pay attention to the metre and the way in which metre and language are accommodated to each other.

3. Comparisons. In my view, the time-honoured comparative exercises still have a place on the pedagogical agenda of the Nineties. The comparative approach has always formed a useful 'handle' to perceptive but inarticulate students. It has certainly brought out many sharp observations around the seminar table in Lund. In addition, comparative questions afford students an opportunity to activate and reapply knowledge they have already acquired. Examples:

a) George Crabbe, *The Village*. Compare Crabbe's attitude to country life to Goldsmith's and Gray's. How would Crabbe defend himself against the accusation that he denigrates simple country folk?

b) Robert Burns, *The Jolly Beggars*. *The Jolly Beggars* would seem to have little in common with poems like Gray's 'Bard' and Ossian's Songs on the one hand and Thomson's *Liberty* and Cowper's poems about oppression on the other – but two popular ideological currents of the late eighteenth century, exemplified in those works, can be clearly discerned in Burns's cantata. Can you name them and quote pertinent passages?

4. Analyses of critical pronouncements. Inviting the reactions of students to opinions expressed by critical and scholarly authorities is another instructive procedure. First, it helps students acquire a rough idea of 'what has been said' about a literary work. Second, it supplies an opportunity to acquaint them with representatives of various critical approaches to literature. Third, giving some thought to the views of established critics develops the critical acumen of students. I admit to a *penchant* for selecting pregnable statements from well-known authors in order to encourage students to think for themselves and learn that even the great may well be challenged. That way, excessive reverence for famous names is curbed. A valuable by-product of such exercises is the realisation that just because 'a lot has been done' in a particular field, that does not necessarily mean that there is no need for a lot more to be. Examples:

a) Emily Brontë, *Wuthering Heights*. '[Catherine's choice between Heathcliff and Edgar Linton] seems to me the pivotal event of the novel, the decisive catalyst of the tragedy; and if this is so, the crux of *Wuthering Heights* must be conceded by even the most remorselessly mythological and mystical of critics to be a social one' (Terry Eagleton, *Myths of Power: A Marxist Study of the Brontës*, p. 101). Are statement and inference acceptable to you?

b) Alfred Tennyson, *In Memoriam A.H.H.* 'The persona fails to find a supernatural "God" because all avenues to the divine are closed, so that he is, in effect, thrown upon his own resources' (Henry Kozicki, 'Meaning in Tennyson's *In Memoriam*'). Do you agree with this description?

5. Appeals to the shrewdness and experience of students in a more general sense. These questions are aimed at the sense and sensibility of 'students as people'. It is no accident that some of the most memorable replies have come from mature students (shaming those who mutter about 'wasting money on people who aren't going to pay it back'). Examples:

a) William Wordsworth, 'The Ruined Cottage'. Wordsworth could have let the story of Margaret end with line 492, or with line 525, but he did not. Those fifty or so lines at the end have a very important function in this tragic narrative. Try to describe it, imagining what the poem would have lost if it had been allowed to end with Margaret's death.

b) George Gordon, Lord Byron, 'The Vision of Judgement'. Besides providing a lovely opportunity for getting even with Southey, the conclusion of 'The Vision' neatly solves the problem of what to do with George III. Why do you think Byron chose this way out of the dilemma?

6. Invitations to speculate. These questions, suitable for the conclusion of a seminar, form a bid for unbounded subjectivism. Despite the sheer self-indulgence they encourage in all participants, answers can sometimes be fruitful as well as entertaining. On several occasions, discussions set off by such questions have reassured me that students have indeed begun to live with the texts, thereby fulfilling my greatest ambition as a teacher. Examples:

a) Jane Austen, *Emma*. An American Austen critic, Marvin Mudrick, has argued that Mr. Knightley is in for a rough time as Emma's husband, that Emma will continue with her dominating ways, and that he will be the unhappy object of her Mrs.-Fixit ideas. Do you share Mudrick's fears? What of the notion, expressed by critics with a Freudian bias, that Emma in marrying Mr. Knightley marries a father-figure?

b) Robert Browning, 'Andrea del Sarto'. If you were to write an 'Apology for Lucrezia', where Andrea's wife would speak in her own defence, what would be the main points in your plaidoyer?

2.3 Works of criticism

Contemplating brief quotations from the works of various commentators, as in the fourth category of study questions, falls short of providing adequate opportunities for criticising critics and learning from them. In the course of each seminar series, I have asked students to read articles, or chapters from books, on central texts. Whenever I have compiled a list of such works and set about supplying them (through bookshops or libraries, or on handouts), I have tried to ensure that they will be worth reading. First of all, they should have something substantial to say about the actual text(s). In addition, they should fulfil at least one of two further criteria: a) they should be seminal works with discernible effects on the labours of successors, and b) they should illustrate a particular approach to the study of literature.

With the magnificent bibliographical aids available to modern scholars, locating and ordering potentially useful materials is an easy job. After ordering, though, it usually takes weeks or months to obtain publications not stocked in one's home library, so it pays to plan well in advance. Once these publications have arrived, a selection must be made. Some may be dismissed altogether; others may prove more suitable as quarries for isolated quotations than as objects of sustained and concentrated study.

One example of category (a) works is Robert Langbaum's classic *The Poetry of Experience: The Dramatic Monologue in Modern Literary Tradition* (1957). Especially the discussions of Browning's dramatic monologues have influenced critical analyses of the relevant texts for decades. Another instance with a similar impact might be quoted, Frank H. Ellis's article 'Gray's *Elegy*: The Biographical Problem in Literary Criticism' (1951). Despite frequent challenges, it has left its mark on virtually all *Elegy* criticism in the second half of the twentieth century. A comment on it from one of my students has stuck in my memory: 'I don't think I buy Ellis's stonecutter, but his article made me feel as if I was reading the *Elegy* for the first time'. What greater accolade could a critic wish for?

When it comes to category (b), several representatives have proved their usefulness with my students. We read Paul de Man's chapters on Wordsworth and Shelley in *The Rhetoric of Romanticism* (1984) alongside a selection of their poems. The book afforded insights into one variant of poststructuralist criticism, and occasional observations struck the students as intriguing. In respect of the pages on Wordsworth's *Prelude* II.237-341 (pp. 89-92 in de Man's book), however, one participant thoughtfully remarked: 'Do you know, I don't think de Man can ever have *watched* a woman breast-feeding her baby'. The discussion immediately entered a much more lively phase.

Two articles on Christina Rossetti supplied a basis for an application of feminist thinking and terminology to her 'sister poems'. We studied Dorothy Mermin's 'Heroic Sisterhood in *Goblin Market*' (1983) and Helena Michie's 'The Battle for Sisterhood: Christina Rossetti's Strategies for Control in Her Sister Poems' (1983). A joint consideration of these two analyses showed that a similar ideological outlook, applied to the same author's texts, need not by any means entail similar results. It supplied welcome evidence to the effect that the qualities and abilities of the individual critic are a matter of overriding importance irrespective of ideological affiliation.

2.4 Tape and video recordings

Audiovisual aids had a galvanising effect on many pedagogical practitioners in the sixties and seventies. While the novelty has now worn off, developments in the field have placed sophisticated equipment as well as plentiful stocks at our disposal. It would be a pity not to make use of them. Not only are a large number of good performances of classic English plays – Shakespeare especially – available on video; many famous novels have been televised and videotaped, and there are great quantities of poetry readings of all kinds. Few poets do as much justice to their own texts as a good actor (Sir Alec Guinness's recordings of T.S. Eliot's poems are, to my mind, vastly superior to Eliot's own); but it would be an act of negligence not to let students listen to, say, Ezra Pound reading from the *Cantos*.

The use of these pedagogical instruments is apt to be time-consuming, though, and it often calls for voluntary pre- or post-seminar sessions. Where such arrangements pose no problems, the benefits can be great. Watching a Shakespeare performance or listening to a recording of *Under Milk Wood* after having devoted plenty of time and effort to the work in question often proves a point that many students and teachers of literature were aware of long before the days of modern theory: the reading experience is not a static or reproducible phenomenon. Not only do different people often react differently to a text; it keeps assuming different shapes in the individual reader's mind, too.

2.5 The collective factor

Still, it is partly thanks to the successive percolation of poststructuralist lines of thought that students have stopped demanding to be told what a particular text 'means'. No longer are replies to such queries copied down and reproduced in examinations (at least not anywhere I know). This liberation from the tyranny of The Best – or, worse, The Correct – Reading is a great boon in present-day literary teaching.

And yet there is such a thing as a collective dimension to the reading experience. People do tend to be similarly affected by a text. Classroom teaching proves it every day. One student, for instance, hits on especially apt words to describe the impact of a poem, a 'character', or a scene, and an expression of approval and relief instantly shows on the faces of all present. Literature could not function as a very special vehicle for human communication if that were not so. Lines of verse, snatches of prose, figures, scenes, incidents – we do not only assimilate them in our own particular ways; we use them to create a sense of mutual understanding and recognition, too. To quote a single example, a passing reference to the tears of young Mrs. Casaubon in

Rome immediately evokes feelings of pity, even tenderness, mixed with vexation at wasted excellence and misguided idealism (provided, of course, one's literary fare has not been restricted to contemporary 'works closely connected with one's own environment'). Access to the fellowship of readers is another blessing conferred by literary study.

Anyone who recognises and appreciates a collective dimension in the study of literature might be expected to be enthusiastic about group projects. Many teachers divide students into study groups, assign different tasks to different groups, and structure a scheme of joint class presentation and discussion. I am sure this often works very well, but I have never done it myself. For one thing, no seminar I have conducted has counted more than 16 participants, not too many for joint discussions throughout. For another, I feel sceptical about the value of any study group that does not evolve and constitute itself on the basis of a commonly felt need and/or wish. Some of my students have formed spontaneous 'groups' between seminars, tackling articles and study questions together. In those cases, the group structure served a purpose and often produced excellent results. It is not, however, a thing I would impose on anybody.

2.6 The question of examination

Special assignments can be valuable in the course of a series of seminars and constitute at least a partial solution to the problem of examination. It is often felt today that traditional written or *viva-voce* examinations are rather unimaginative forms of accounting for knowledge acquired, and that student energy might be more usefully applied to assignment work than to pre-exam cramming. Instead, it is proposed that students should, for example, submit term papers or present the results of individual (or 'group') assignments for the benefit of their fellow seminar participants. Several advantages are attached to such a proceeding. Among others, the course could be made to comprise more material, all of which would in some way be made available to all students; besides, essay-writing and communicative skills would be practised.

The implementation of such an examination principle, however, requires constant attendance and loyal seminar participation on the part of all students, which might not always be feasible. How, for instance, is one to deal with a student who (quoting good reasons, no doubt) misses a number of seminars and then presents a scanty paper, showing little honest effort? Fail her (nearly all my students are women), demand better things, and put in hours of extra supervision and marking of no benefit to the other participants? It is probably wise to lay down certain qualitative criteria from the start and stick to them.

My personal preference is still vivas with one student at a time. After an initial check in order to establish that all important texts (including critical works) have been attentively studied, the student is free to address any relevant topic or topics in the course of an informal chat. Such talks have sometimes seen the distinction between examiner and examinee, between teacher and student, evaporate bit by bit, leaving two people quietly exulting together over words that stayed with both long after the session was over.

Feminist Theory/Pedagogy in the 1990s

Suzette Henke, University of Louisville, USA

One of the most exciting aspects of teaching Feminist Theory and Women's Studies at the end of this century is the relative curricular innovation possible in a field that is still in process. Those of us who came of pedagogical age in the 1970s can remember a time when Women's Studies was an untried discipline – a field that seemed suspect to institutions and individual professors alike. As late as 1975, I had to go before a special departmental curricular committee at the University of Virginia to plead for a course in Modern Women Authors. 'You want to teach a whole course devoted to women?' one colleague queried, somewhat incredulously. 'But *why*?' Ten years later, in the mid-1980s, I found myself making a similar case for the teaching of Feminist Theory. By this time, however, student demand and theoretical expansion of English Studies had caught up with my own interests. Having spent a semester reading Feminist Theory at the Camargo Foundation in southern France, I returned to the United States eager to share feminist explorations with a graduate student constituency clamoring for enlightenment.

Herein lies the excitement and the challenge, as well as the difficulty, of teaching Feminist Theory/Women's Studies. The discipline is as new as our own always-already in-progress expertise. For the generation of women scholars trained in the mid 1970s, Women's Studies has emerged as a field constantly burgeoning and always being pioneered. Having received doctorates largely in 'White-Male-Eurocentric' studies, we have spent the past two decades rediscovering, re-visioning, and reconceptualizing literature on the margins. Embracing a decentered and destabilized subject-position, we have felt continually vertiginous. As Elaine Showalter notes, feminists have moved from fragile, embryonic beginnings in the teaching of courses labeled Images of Women, explorative of male and female writing across centuries; to a concentration on gynocriticism, focussed on writing by and about women; to a more expansive interrogation not only of female literary texts, but of a feminist methodology that has acquired legitimacy in academic institutions only within the last ten years (Women's Time, Women's Space). Now a decade old, the teaching of Feminist Theory is still the 'new kid on the block' – a pedagogical process that necessarily involves learning and exchange for the instructor, as well as for the students, all of whom are struggling to understand dense theoretical frameworks that, as often as not, contradict one another at the same time that they challenge unexamined master narratives of the critical establishment. (The question of feminist pedagogy has been eloquently and extensively treated in Culley and Portuges 1985).

In the age of poststructuralism and deconstruction, Feminist Theory has rapidly gained credibility as a radical discourse fashionably positioned on the margins of literary interrogation. But theory and practice fold back on one another in the nature of a Möbius strip, perpetually challenging traditional hierarchical arrangements of cultural discourse, power and domination. The danger, of course, is a radical but unsuspecting adoption of what Foucault would label a 'reverse discourse', privileging as 'politically correct' precisely those marginalized voices that have traditionally been silenced in academic institutions. As women struggle to speak and to be heard, it seems difficult to purvey a pedagogical practice that refuses precisely those hierarchical models of mastery and hegemony called into question by feminist/Marxist interrogation. How, one wonders, can praxis correspond to theory? How can an introductory seminar be open to a polyphonous discourse that refuses to embrace western, patriarchal practices of mastery everywhere found in academic training?

In the fall semester, 1990, I offered a course on Feminist Theory at the graduate level at the State University of New York at Binghamton. I felt fortunate that the class was small – about a dozen students – and that we were able to meet for three hours every week, on a Tuesday evening, which allowed for some informality and flexibility. The objective of the seminar was to offer an introduction to Feminist Theory, with particular emphasis on Anglo-American and French psychoanalytic approaches. The class was organized non-hierarchically, with students choosing to introduce the material and to be responsible for discussion each evening. Pedagogical strategies focussed around issues raised by the participants and took whatever direction seemed germane to the group. A colloquium scheduled at the end of term gave the seminarians a chance to share research ideas with one another and to get peer responses to their final projects.

What struck me about this class, which was, perhaps by chance, all female, was the variety of agendas that participants brought forward. Whereas other offerings in the curriculum are usually self-bounded and autotelic, Women's Studies courses in general and Feminist Theory courses in particular appeal to deeply-buried emotional needs that students bring to the study of literature. They desire a literary practice that will somehow speak to them directly – that will allow utterance to a voice that has consistently been silenced by the dominant discourses of the institution. They approach the class with inchoate, sometimes unconscious needs, and tacitly seek a critical practice that will magically forge an alliance between reading and feminine experience. The demands are high, and many are so repressed or obscured that the dialogue emerging can at times seem irrelevant, digressive, chaotic, or uncontrolled. One of the challenges of feminist pedagogy is to expand the possibilities of discourse in the classroom – to allow space for subjective utterances that have heretofore been considered illegitimate in academic fora. Margins there must be, perhaps, to demarcate areas of interest and avoid the pitfalls of amorphous 'consciousness-raising' that strays well beyond the boundaries of literary study. But then, if we do feel committed to an unbounded text, to the gradual dissolution of those subject/object distinctions foisted upon us by New Criticism, should we move in the direction of an 'unbounded classroom' and dissolve all barriers between private experience and public discourse? At what point does the seminar cease to be academically appropriate and degenerate into group therapy? Each instructor/participant must grapple with this question, and the answer may prove different for every seminar, professor, and group interaction. The most difficult task might simply be a genuine commitment to non-hierarchical practice within a classroom setting. The teaching of Feminist Theory and deconstruction should, I suspect, always prove a humbling pedagogical experience precisely because there is no set body of material to be mastered and professed.

One of the primary issues involved in constructing a seminar on Feminist Theory is that of choosing texts. Considering the wealth of material available, I cannot imagine teaching this kind of course from a single anthology. In the past decade, textual possibilities have proliferated exponentially. In the 1970s, I made abundant use of Susan Koppelman Cornillon's anthology entitled *Images of Women*, as well as Josephine Donovan's theoretical work on *Feminist Literary Criticism*. In the 1980s, I tended to rely more heavily on Elaine Showalter's *Feminist Criticism: Essays on Women, Literature and Theory*, as well as on *New French Feminisms*, compiled by Elaine Marks and Isabelle de Courtivron. Unfortunately, these excellent collections now seem relatively dated – too eclectic and unfocussed in their presentation of Anglo-American criticism, and far too choppy and fragmented in their French feminist offerings. And so, salvaging Showalter's two classic essays on 'Toward a Feminist Poetics' and 'Feminist Criticism in the Wilderness', I decided to choose, for the first two weeks of the course, selections from Gayle Greene and Coppelia Kahn's *Making a Difference* and from Judith Newton and Deborah Rosenfelt's *Feminist Criticism and Social Chance*. I asked each of the twelve students to prepare a ten-minute presentation on one of a dozen essays: 'Feminist Scholarship' by Greene and Kahn, 'Varieties of Feminist Criticism' by Sydney Janet Kaplan, 'The Politics of Language' by Nelly Furman, 'Inscribing Femininity: French Theories of the Feminine' by Ann Rosalind Jones, 'Mind Mother: Psychoanalysis and Feminism' by Judith Kegan Gardiner, 'Pandora's Box: Subjectivity, Class and Sexuality' by Cora Kaplan,

'Constructing the Subject: Deconstructing the Text' by Catherine Belsey, 'Ideology and the Cultural Production of Gender' by Michelle Barrett, 'An Overview of Lesbian Feminist Criticism' by Bonnie Zimmerman, 'Black Women Writers' by Susan Willis, 'Toward a Black Feminist Criticism' by Barbara Smith, and 'Notorious Signs, Feminist Criticism and Literary Tradition' by Adrienne Munich. During the first two weeks of intense immersion, some participants complained about the sheer quantity of material. Later in the course, however, they returned to the initial essays with a sense of familiarity and gratitude. These texts laid the groundwork for future study, and the class was now eager to explore the feminist critical revolution.

We began with an examination of current trends in Anglo-American criticism. The students had already read Showalter's essays, as well as those by Greene and Kahn, Furman, and Belsey. But the first volume of Sandra Gilbert and Susan Gubar's *No Man's Land* proved somewhat of a disappointment. It offered a feminist literary history that at times seemed reductive. By using an exclusively feminist lens to review twentieth-century canonical texts, Gilbert and Gubar had apparently thrust some literary giants into an uncomfortably Procrustean bed. Certainly, one might appreciate Virginia Woolf, Kate Chopin, Edith Wharton and Willa Cather without jettisoning male contemporaries such as James Joyce and Ernest Hemingway. Rather than simply reporting on an ostensible sex-role struggle in the early twentieth century, Gilbert and Gubar had declared gender war and were passionately reporting from the front lines. Having myself spent the past decade re-visioning the work of James Joyce, I was quick to point out the limitations of their assessment of this particular author as chauvinist guardian of the male-dominated *patrius sermo*. I suggested that a feminist might simultaneously be a resisting reader and an appreciative one, and pointed to my own book, *James Joyce and the Politics of Desire*, as an antidote. At two different junctures in *No Man's Land*, Gilbert and Gubar spell the name of Gerty MacDowell with different orthographies: Gerty MacDowell/Gertie McDowell. Only the first is correct, and the second manages to introduce errors in both given and family names. If feminism is to be recognized as a powerful and revolutionary critical ideology, then one must certainly take pains to avoid such examples of scholarly slippage.

Virginia Woolf's *A Room of One's Own* provided welcome relief from the controversy. The students unanimously agreed with Woolf's trenchant critique of the Victorian 'angel in the house' and happily embraced her philosophy of androgynous reading/writing/criticism. Woolf, the mother of us all, offered a voice of reason and mediation across the uncharted terrain of no man's land. And her later polemical tract *Three Guineas* struck the students as more radical, and thus potentially more useful to contemporary political praxis.

Toril Moi's *Sexual/Textual Politics* begins with a salute to Virginia Woolf by way of admonishing Anglo-American critics for their misunderstanding of the postmodern dimensions of Woolf's canon. Most women in the class felt offended by Moi's articulation of Anglo-American criticism in terms of earlier views expressed by Kate Millett, Ellen Moers, Elaine Showalter, Annette Kolodny and Myra Jehlen. American critics, Moi charges, have approached Woolf from a realist standpoint that obscures her lyrical, poetic, and semiotic experimentation. Why, I wondered, had Moi chosen to ignore the groundbreaking work of critics like Jane Marcus, Madeline Moore, and Ellen Rosenman? In the preparation of this volume, she had apparently stopped reading Anglo-American criticism around the year 1980. Moi covered the American scene through the 1970s: she could excoriate Kate Millett's 'eloquent, angry indictments' of male authors (Moi 1985:30) and chide the author for her failure to acknowledge debts to the work of Katharine M. Rogers and Mary Ellmann. The only American feminist Moi admires is Mary Ellmann, who safely confined her argument to initial interrogations of the pervasive sex-role stereotypes that have traditionally structured critical response to the literary canon. My seminar students felt incensed by Moi's cavalier dismissal of Anglo-American Feminist Theory. Yet here is the paradox: this year's leading edge article, incorporated into a book that is stalled several years at press, may simply be outdated by the time it sees print. Five years ago, I rejoiced at the publication of Moi's introductory study. Now I was forced to defend it on the basis of publication lag-time. Moi's work could not begin to cope with the explosion of germinal texts during the last ten years: works like Alice Jardine's *Gynesis*, Nancy Chodorow's *Reproduction of Mothering*, Maggie Humm's *Feminist Criticism*, Josephine Donovan's *Feminist Theory*, Carol Gilligan's *In a Different Voice*, Barbara Christian's *Black Feminist Criticism*, Trinh Minh-ha's *Woman, Native, Other*, Jane Gallop's *Reading Lacan*, McConnell-Ginet, Borker and Furman's *Women and Language in Literature and Society* and Rita Felski's *Beyond Feminist Aesthetics* – to name only a few crucial books that have come out in the past decade. The field of Women's Studies has developed at such a prodigious rate that most of us feel humbled by the sheer breadth and expansiveness of this critical endeavour. Jane Marcus has argued against Moi quite eloquently in her own speculative essay 'Daughters of Anger/Material Girls: Con/Textualizing Feminist Criticism' – a piece now collected and edited by Regina Barreca in *Last Laughs*. And so I turned my students' attention to this critique and carried on.

I had actually assigned Moi's *Sexual/Textual Politics* not for its commentary on Anglo-American feminism but for what I had thought an excellent introduction to the new French feminisms of Hélène Cixous, Luce Irigaray, and Julia Kristeva. Here, again, the class felt cheated, as it were, by what they described as Moi's 'slash-and-burn' approach. Rather than finding illuminations they cringed at her tacit vituperation in discussions of Simone de Beauvoir, Hélène Cixous and Luce Irigaray. Only Julia Kristeva, with her theoretical emphasis on linguistic interrogation, could pass muster in Moi's harshly skeptical roll-call. But even she had been examined and found wanting. Under the auspices of Toril Moi, the students had been escorted through a maze of current theory only to be led to a cul-de-sac, a blind alley in which extant critical strategies were uniformly trashed. Where could the aspiring feminist critic search for positive enlightenment?

I understood the class's disappointment with Moi, but I felt startled to realize that these eager disciples were entirely unfamiliar with the classic texts that had founded the current feminist movement. No one had read Simone de Beauvoir's *The Second Sex*, Kate Millett's *Sexual Politics*, Germaine Greer's *The Female Eunuch*, or Robin Morgan's edited collection, *Sisterhood is Powerful*. Because they were approaching Feminist Theory as an extant ideology, they could not appreciate the sense of wonder and amazement that characterized those first glimmerings of a revolutionary movement that burst onto the horizon in the early 1970s. They missed the thrill of discovery that had galvanized so many of us at the dawn of the second wave of the Women's Movement. And they had no critical/historical context from which to assess Moi's survey of *Sexual/Textual Politics*. There simply wasn't time to insist, in one semester, that they read all the influential and groundbreaking texts by our feminist foremothers. Such an assignment would constitute an entirely different course – one entitled, perhaps, Classics of Feminist Theory. *This* class was pressed to move on to Chris Weedon's *Feminist Practice and Poststructuralist Theory*.

Again, I felt taken aback by the students' response to a book that had intrigued last year's seminar. Whereas an earlier group praised Weedon's treatment of feminism and poststructuralism, the more jaded class of 1990 expressed a good bit of frustration and annoyance. One student complained about Weedon's relentless repetitions, observing that her entire volume could have been summarized in a few succinct paragraphs. After all, Weedon's most salient points center around her conviction that 'poststructuralism proposes a subjectivity which is precarious, contradictory and in process, constantly being reconstituted in discourse each time we think or speak', and that 'feminist poststructuralism insists that forms of subjectivity are produced historically and change with shifts in the wide range of discursive fields which constitute them' (Weedon 1987:33). Only one student seemed to appreciate Weedon's densely-argued analysis. A book which I had previously considered indispensable to an understanding of Feminist Theory and the construction of the subject had gone the way of *Sexual/Textual Politics*. At this point, the students were anxious to tackle headier stuff. We had already spent six weeks reading books and essays *about* Feminist Theory. Wasn't it time to move on to more primary texts on feminism and psychoanalysis? Julia Kristeva, Luce Irigaray, and Hélène Cixous were at the very heart of the syllabus.

Kristeva, Cixous, and Irigaray, however, do not make for easy or accessible reading. In retrospect, I realize that I simply assigned too much reading, asking the students to assimilate enormously difficult theoretical structures in a highly compressed time-frame. My greatest regret has to do with our attempt to cover a majority of the essays collected in Toril Moi's *Kristeva Reader* in the course of a single evening. Although I chose limited selections from this anthology, I had managed to forget or repress the ponderousness of the material under examination. How could a novice plough through the linguistic complexities of 'The System and the Speaking Subject' and 'Word, Dialogue and Novel' from *Desire in Language*, along with Kristeva's classic essays on 'Women's Time' and 'Stabat Mater' and substantially the whole of *Revolution in Poetic Language*, condensed into an illusively short essay of the same name? This was not to mention Kristeva's most recent work on 'The True-Real' and 'Freud and Love', which apparently went unread by all but the instructor. The student introducing the material that evening offered a mercifully lucid explanation of Kristeva's theory of phenotext and genotext, along with an excellent interpretation of the Kristevan notion of a semiotic *chora*. But most members of the seminar balked. Guiltily, and with compunctions, I suggested that we carry our discussion of Kristeva over to the next week – by which time almost everyone had forgotten or repressed their reading of seven days before. Kristeva had eluded many of the earnest disciples of Feminist Theory, and I myself, like the Stabat Mater, was drenched in remorse for having gotten so carried away by my own enthusiasm.

The good news was that, after Kristeva, Luce Irigaray seemed positively accessible. The students were somewhat mystified by the first and last chapters of *This Sex Which Is Not One*, but enjoyed Irigaray's notion of feminine sexual/genital multiplicity and the kind of innovative discourse that might be associated with an attempt to 'write the body' in creative literature. Understandably, they raised pertinent questions. What, finally, is *écriture féminine*? Do women write differently from men; and if so, should their/our exploration of sexual/textual difference be ascribed to nature and gender, or to socialization and culture? Many of the women in the seminar expressed vociferous opposition to Irigaray's notion that female sexuality might in some way open up new, avant-garde styles of lyricism and semiotic rhythms. After all, didn't such theories thrust women back into those essentialist categories we had so passionately tried to eschew during the first wave of feminist political agitation? Had Irigaray simply reverted to essentialist categories of feminine difference that could be used to reinforce entrenched and denigrating stereotypes? These issues inaugurated heated debate between those who felt offended by Irigaray's sex-linked celebration of *parler-femme* ('speaking-as-a-woman') and those who found her theories wonderfully suggestive, inspiring, and liberating. One student, in fact, produced a fascinating final paper analyzing Edith Wharton's much-neglected novel *Summer* under the auspices of Irigaray's analytic techniques.

Hélène Cixous' *Sorties*, in Betsy Wing's translation of *The Newly Born Woman*, was somewhat less successful, since by now, the two camps had become firmly entrenched, and one group objected to still another French feminist paean to the *jouissance* involved in 'writing the body' through *écriture féminine*. One participant, herself a writer, protested that the image of woman writing with breast-milk and menstrual blood is just as offensive as that of a male/macho penile/pen trajectory. Cixous passionately exclaims: 'Her rising: is not erection. But diffusion. Not the shaft. The vessel. Let her write!' (Cixous 1985:88). All could appreciate the euphoric lyricism of Cixous' style and revel in its revolutionary rhetoric. But should we take literally the tenor of Cixous' metaphorical outbursts? Surprisingly, the class most appreciated the bits of feminist analysis buried in Cixous' ecstatic tract. They enjoyed her textual commentaries on Kleist and on Shakespeare. But why, they wondered, did she restrict such interpretive forays to male, rather than female authors?

The course ended with a discussion of Jane Gallop's *Feminism and Psychoanalysis* and with individual analyses of three (post)modern texts by women: Djuna Barnes's *Nightwood*, Angela Carter's *The Bloody Chamber*, and Toni Morrison's *Beloved*. With delight and astonishment, every member of the class discovered that her own approach to literary criticism had been radically, unequivocally altered in the course of the semester. The students, to their own amazement, had begun to approach literary texts with an entirely new critical sensibility. All had changed utterly by fifteen weeks of immersion in contemporary Feminist Theory.

Was the seminar successful? I would say that, despite all its trials and errors, this course was, in the end, germinal and profoundly transformative. The pedagogical methods had been democratic and non-hierarchical, the modes of revelation sometimes epiphanic. In our last colloquium, the students shared their papers-in-progress with one another, and the results were impressive. They were writing wonderfully perceptive, incisive, and theoretically sophisticated essays.

For this professor, at least, the seminar in Feminist Theory proved enormously gratifying. Any experimental course of this nature will present unexpected challenges. One must stumble ahead with gusto, despite the plethora of problems and mistakes that adhere to the task of pioneering new educational strategies for the 1990s. As Feminist Theory constantly evolves, so must our pedagogical praxis. Because the field is too explosive ever to be mastered, we must abandon the notion of professorial authority contingent on scholarly management of more traditional fields. The most exciting aspect of this kind of project is its groundbreaking assumptions of perpetually shifting positionality. We can only remain humble in the face of such revolutionary, life-transforming possibilities.

APPENDIX: Course programme for Feminist Theory, Fall 1990

8/28 Introduction
9/4   Gayle Greene & Coppelia, *Making a Difference* (Reports)
9/11 Judith Newton & Deborah Rosenfelt, *Feminist Criticism and Social Change* (Reports)

FEMINISM/MODERNISM

9/18 Sandra Gilbert & Susan Gubar, *No Man's Land*, Vol. 1
9/25 Virginia Woolf, *A Room of One's Own*
      Recommended: *Three Guineas*
10/2 Virginia Woolf, *Mrs. Dalloway*; Moi 1-18; Waugh 88-125
10/9 Toril Moi, *Sexual/Textual Politics*; Moi, in Brennan 189-205
10/16 Chris Weedon, *Feminist Practice and Poststructuralist Theory*; Spivak, in Brennan 206-23

FEMINISM/PSYCHOANALYSIS

10/23 Julia Kristeva, *The Kristeva Reader* (Selections)
      Recommended: Elizabeth Grosz, *Sexual Subversions*
10/30 Luce Irigaray, *This Sex Which Is Not One*.
      Recommended: Grosz, *Sexual Subversions*; Brennan 106-37
11/6 Djuna Barnes, *Nightwood*
11/13 Jane Gallop, *Feminism and Psychoanalysis: The Daughter's Seduction*: 'Moving Backwards,' in Brennan 27-39

FEMINISM/POSTMODERNISM

11/20 Rita Felski, *Beyond Feminist Aesthetics*
      Wright, in Brennan 141-52
11/27 Linda Nicholson, *Feminism/Postmodernism*
      Angela Carter, *The Bloody Chamber*
      Recommended: Waugh, *Feminine Fictions* 1-33
12/4 Toni Morrison, *Beloved*
12/11 SEMINAR: Feminist Theory and Literary Criticism
      Presentation of Student Papers

Teaching 'Woman as Monster': The Growth of a Project

Dorrit Einersen and Ingeborg Nixon,
University of Copenhagen, Denmark

The idea of tracing the theme of 'woman as monster' in (primarily) English literature was conceived by Ingeborg Nixon in 1984, discussed intermittently by the two of us during the spring of 1985 and launched in the autumn term.

Our preconception was that it might be difficult to find sufficient material – texts and representations in art – to fill a whole term, but in actual fact two terms were barely sufficient. This was primarily due to the class, who were so engaged in the subject that they suggested numerous texts and cut up their families' newspapers to exemplify alluring, dangerous, snake-like women, mermaids, Medusas and man-like viragoes.

Our idea was to start with Anglo-Saxon literature and trace the theme from the beginnings of English literature – Grendel's monstrous mother – through the numerous medieval versions of 'the loathly lady' motif (Chaucer's *The Wife of Bath's Tale*, Gower's *The Tale of Florent*, *Sir Gawain and Dame Ragnell*, *King Henry*) via Spenser's Duessa in *The Faerie Queene* and Shakespeare's Lady Macbeth, Goneril and Regan to Keats's *Lamia* and Coleridge's *Christabel*, Edgar Allan Poe's *Ligeia* and the ambiguous governess in Henry James's *The Turn of the Screw*.

A side-effect of starting with early literature was to open the students' eyes to connections between ancient and medieval, partly mythical underlying conceptions, and the imaginative literature of for instance the Romantic period. It was frequently necessary to go into general period characteristics and discuss genre requirements, and these literary-cultural backgrounds were avidly devoured – whereas it is often the case that presentations of literary-cultural surveys to students can be felt as duty rather than pleasure, hard facts rather than stimulation of the imagination.

When we reached the twentieth century, the students were able to contribute widely and draw parallels between literature and films, TV-serials and magazine and newspaper advertisements. The main texts we studied in depth were Sylvia Townsend Warner's *Lolly Willowes* (1978), Walter de la Mare's 'Seaton's Aunt' (1942), Elizabeth Jane Howard's 'Three Miles Up' (1979),

William Sansom's 'A Woman Seldom Found' (1956), Fay Weldon's *Puffball* (1980) and *The Life and Loves of a She-Devil* (1983), and Susan Hill's *The Woman in Black* (1983), which was suggested by one of the students.

Our common background within English literature, primarily the medieval period (Dorrit Einersen) and the nineteenth century (Ingeborg Nixon) made class discussions also discussions between the two of us, and we found it important as well as stimulating to co-teach, a form of teaching which is unfortunately becoming increasingly rare because of its cost in resources.

Apart from literature we included in the course some books on culture and art. One book that we found particularly useful was Nina Auerbach's *Woman and the Demon* (1982), a fascinating study of the duality of woman in the Victorian period: the virtuous angel in the house and the countertype, the demonic, destructive or fallen woman luring man away from the narrow path. Perhaps most interesting was Auerbach's demonstration of demonic power in seemingly powerless, passive Victorian women in literature and art.

Another highly stimulating book on representations of women in art was Edwin Mullins's *The Painted Witch* (1985), which uncovered men's fears of women's power and attempts to reduce women to manageable stereotypes. Mullins's analyses of paintings from different periods were balanced, wittily phrased and implicitly feminist in intent.

The Dutch art historian Bram Dijkstra's recent book on *Idols of Perversity: Fantasies of Feminine Evil in Fin-de-Siècle Culture* (1986) provided fascinating perspectives on mythical figures like Lilith, the sirens, Medusa and Lamia, and was a gold mine of valuable background material not only to an understanding of cultural and literary developments and themes in paintings and writings of the 1890s but to preceding and later representations of perverse, destructive women.

Our common lack of a solid background within psychology was keenly felt. This was a field into which we feared to tread. We did, however, include in our discussions extracts from Karen Horney's *Feminine Psychology* (1967), Wolfgang Lederer's *The Fear of Women* (1968), Simone de Beauvoir's *The Second Sex* (1953) and Eva Figes's *Patriarchal Attitudes* (1970), and we were so fortunate as to have one student in the class who was well-versed in Jungian psychology. She contributed greatly to our understanding of Keats's *Lamia*, and she unravelled archetypal patterns as well as obscure alchemic references in Arthur Machen's *The White People* (1949).

Another student was deeply fascinated by Richard Adams's novel *The Girl in a Swing* (1980) and by the film based on this novel. She gave an enthusiastic and illuminating talk on parallels between the female protagonist of the novel and mythical Lilith- and Lamia-figures.

A number of exam papers, oral exams and theses (on, for instance, Richard Adams's *The Girl in a Swing* and Fay Weldon's *The Life and Loves of a She-Devil*) materialized in the wake of the course, so, as regards efficiency and increase in the number of examinations passed, even Bertel Haarder (our Minister of Education) might have been content with the result.

One of the external examiners at an oral exam was so fascinated by the theme as it was illustrated in Romantic poetry and paintings that she could not stop discussing it for half an hour after the exam was supposed to have ended. She expressed envy that it was possible for us to take up such a broad theme and read not just a few dispersed and disparate modern novels but a proliferation of varied texts, old and new. Where she worked – at Copenhagen Business School – such a course would be unthinkable, as it may indeed soon turn out to be at university level as the new Danish three-year B.A. study requirements become increasingly rigid and limiting.

During the two terms we taught the course we frequently discussed collecting the diversified material we had used in the form of annotated texts (old and new) and selected passages from texts as well as illustrations from art of the theme of 'woman as monster', but the proliferation of material has so far proved too overwhelming and our burden of teaching and exams too heavy to allow us the requisite time to carry out this project. Only two shorter articles on female monsters have appeared as yet: 'Woman as Monster: Virago and Lamia' (Einersen and Nixon 1987), where we concentrated on the man-like, grotesque, huge anti-woman, the virago, and on the snake-like, alluring, lurkingly dangerous and destructive superfeminine woman, the Lamia-type; and 'Woman as Monster: Duality and Ambiguity in the Female Image' (Einersen and Nixon 1989), which focuses on the ambiguous, multi-faceted representations of women in English literature.

However, we have not given up hope of finding the time to categorize and annotate an anthology of texts and paintings illustrating the theme of 'woman as monster' through the centuries. Alternatively, we have discussed treating one or two types of 'monster woman' in much greater depth than we have done so far. In any case, the two terms we spent on the theme with our exceptionally active and motivated students will remain a golden memory of ideal interaction between teachers and students engaged in a joint quest for new insight and illumination.

Historical Materialism and the Literary Text: A Marxist Approach to Degree Teaching

Christopher Hampton, Polytechnic of Central London, UK

Any application of Marxist critical theory to the teaching of English literature at the tertiary (or secondary) level would need first of all to define the materialist *grounds* on which the theory functions – its dialectic of interaction between theory on the one hand and what Marx calls 'the this-sidedness' of thinking, the 'human-sensuous activity' of social practice (Marx 1975:422) by which the senses themselves 'become *theoreticians* in their immediate praxis' (Marx 1975:352). That is axiomatic. And of course the concept of historical materialism, by which 'the mode of production of material life conditions the general process of social, political and intellectual life' (Marx 1975:425), is fundamental in its challenge to all forms of idealism and the ideologies that issue from them. So what has first to be established is the insistence of the Marxian dialectic: that all ideas, values, beliefs – however seemingly 'natural' and 'permanent' – are in reality 'historical and transitory products' of the changing social process that shapes people's lives; of the struggle for 'rights', 'needs' and 'living conditions' which Marx identified historically as the *class* struggle. In this sense, all *cultural* manifestations in society are to be defined in the context of 'the collective struggle to wrest a Realm of Freedom from the Realm of Necessity' (Marx 1977:820) – which is itself determined not by individual will but by 'the contradictions of material life' (Marx 1975:426). And it was Marx's immediate task, in applying his materialist dialectic to the ways in which capitalism functioned as a system of production, to *unmask* its contradictions in order to provide grounds, material *pre*-conditions from which to build his revolutionary theory of social transformation for the liberation of men and women from the oppressive, alienating conditions of a class-divided society. For Marx – and thus crucially for any theorist of literature who claims to be a Marxist – it is only when people have become fully conscious of the nature of the conditions they are controlled by, that 'the development of

human energy' as 'an end in itself, the true Realm of Freedom', can begin –
precisely because it is an *illusory* freedom that does not have 'the Realm of
Necessity as its basis' (Marx 1977:820).

The *problem*, and the *challenge*, of the Marxist approach to literature is
therefore a problem of explaining the interaction of theory and practice, the
application of theory *to* practice – of demonstrating the ways in which historical materialism and its dialectic methodology can influence, play upon, and
transform the *praxis* of the literary text.

That is to put it at its simplest. But since one cannot assume familiarity with
the *process* of the interaction, one has to take it further. Indeed, it is necessary
to assume *unfamiliarity* with the methods on which Marxian theory is based,
and to take as little as possible of what it functions in terms of for granted.
One has to begin, that is, from the premiss that most students are likely to be
deeply conditioned and influenced by the ideology of the system of liberal
capitalism that pervades European society at all levels – the unexamined belief
that we live in a social order that encourages, protects and advances the
interests of the individual in terms of freedom of choice, freedom of speech
and freedom of action, even though these freedoms are mostly determined by
economic conditions which remain a privilege rather than a right and are based
on a division of labour which leaves a great many citizens culturally deprived.

The immediate problem for the Marxist theorist is therefore to break through
the conditioning barriers that persist and the assumptions they encourage; to
make it possible for students to step back from their conditioning so that they
can begin to recognize, and actively contest, the contradictory process they are
involved in. And this is a problem of identifying the forces that lie behind the
ideological facade – the material conditions that determine the grounds of
literary production on the principle that literary-cultural activity is itself an
ideological product, even though, at its most penetrating, it can also become
a dialectic presence, a subversive critical energy and a resilient voice for
change, as in the work of writers like Shakespeare, Milton, Blake, Shelley,
Dickens, not to mention great Europeans such as Balzac, Tolstoy, Ibsen,
Thomas Mann and Brecht.

So the primary step is to get the students to start thinking (and writing)
dialectically – looking for the (often hidden) contradictions in the most
apparently innocent statements, and, bringing them to the surface, to register
in the discrepancies between theory and practice the social dislocations they
reflect, as symptomatic of underlying conditions, a division of labour which
continues to separate manual-material work from almost all forms of
intellectual activity. In this sense, the divisive system of capitalist production,
whereby literary activity thrives upon the economic leisure provided by
millions whose labour produces the wealth which makes this leisure possible,
has to be clearly defined, identified and understood, not only in theoretical
terms, but in the examination of the ideas, values and beliefs embodied (or

implicit) in literary texts – by reading and responding to these texts at all levels, both verbally, in the dialogic conditions of debate, and through writing about them. And perhaps we might do well to keep on reminding ourselves, adopting the cautious detachment of a thinker like Walter Benjamin, that significant works of art 'owe their existence not only to the efforts of the great minds and talents that have created them, but also to the anonymous toil of their contemporaries'; and, as Benjamin adds, with asperity, that 'There is no document of civilization which is not at the same time a document of barbarism' (Benjamin 1973:258).

The aim is to incite responses from students on issues of literary judgement which will acknowledge and make active use of what often remains implicit (and even repressed) in the text. To this end, Marx's fundamental principle – that philosophy should be concerned not with contemplation of the world but rather with how to change it – needs to be firmly spelled out, defined and discussed as a dialectic, an interactive relationship between 'the reality and power of thought' (Marx 1975:422) and 'the practical energy of people' (Marx 1975:354), the theoretical process and the 'this-sidedness' of human activity (Marx 1975:422). In other words, while on the one hand theory provides the indispensable framework for understanding, it is the forms of practice – the social uses of language, the ways in which pressure is put upon the system in the interstices of ideology, the *praxis* of living – that give theory its substance, content, meaning. Get *this* across to the students, and literary criticism must cease to be mere critical analysis or close-reading of a text to become a wider critical awareness of the historical-cultural contexts within which literature itself functions as a product – what Raymond Williams has defined as cultural materialism: 'the analysis of all forms of signification, including quite centrally writing, within the actual means and conditions of production' (Williams 1983:210).

Once this has been established – and students will need to be continually encouraged to discuss, write and think through its implications for themselves, both in the seminar-group and in their reading of crucial texts – we can then proceed to its application by looking at texts of many different kinds to illuminate the underlying issues and to define the ways in which ideological assumptions can be seen to be at work *on* the text, as on the *reader* of the text.

The manner in which I would envisage the Marxist agenda working within the limits of a degree course in English which covers a diverse range of theory – liberal-humanist, formalist, structuralist and poststructuralist – must of course depend upon the way in which it is organized. At the Polytechnic of Central London I had the good fortune to be involved from the start in the development of a radical course embodying the interconnections of theory and practice as 'literature in context', which was eventually validated by the Council for National Academic Awards. I was therefore in a position to insist that in the first and second years of this four-year course in English (plus a foreign language) there should be units strategically placed within the study-sequence to enable the teacher to generate the theoretical principles of historical materialism and its methods of approach to the literary text as a challenge to other forms of discourse and as a means of establishing the grounds on which Marxist theory could proceed to demonstrate Williams's insistence upon 'the inescapable materiality of works of art' (Williams 1977:162). These units could then be followed up, should the student wish, with an option in the fourth year on *Marxism in Britain*, to be chosen at the end of the second year, immediately before the year abroad.

What was crucial here was the interaction between one unit (now module) and another – the fact that the students should be introduced to a major course on Marxist cultural theory *after* they had been through courses on modernist and liberal-humanist theory and *their* application to the text. For this made it possible to define the perspectives and distinctions more sharply. The course (*Culture and Society: Theory and Practice*) involves continual movement between the theoretical process – Marx, Lukacs, Gramsci, Marcuse, Benjamin and the Frankfurt School, and Marxists in post-war Britain – and certain chosen twentieth-century texts, including Conrad, Auden, Orwell, Grassic Gibbon, Eliot, Brecht, Beckett, Bond and Trevor Griffiths. This runs parallel with another course, *Renaissance Poetry and Drama*, which examines the problems of political, social and ideological change in the Elizabethan-Jacobean age through the work of Sidney, Spenser, Marlowe, Jonson, Middleton and Shakespeare. And in the second year there are three courses which extend the materialist methodology – *Puritanism and Colonialism* (Donne; Milton as revolutionary poet writing in defence of the English Commonwealth both before and after its defeat; the colonialist expansion of England, as reflected in *The Tempest* and the work of Forster and Fanon) in the first semester; and *Nineteenth-Century Industrialism and Its Critics* (Marx, Darwin, Dickens, Gaskell, Browning, Arnold, Morris) running parallel with *Romanticism and Revolution* (Blake to Shelley and Byron) in the second semester.

Each of these seminar-based courses involves a movement in and out of specific texts, and will (with any luck) have demonstrated the fact that no text is ever 'innocent', 'autonomous', 'independent', outside history; and that what teacher and student in their act of collaborative interchange are attempting is 'the transformation of passive contemplative consciousness into active, critical consciousness' (Said 1983:232).

Of course one has to guard against the danger of theory becoming a kind of 'ideological trap' (Said 1983:241). And it is precisely the function of the dialectic to *resist* such closure, the abstract, generalising process that dislocates theory from practice and (by-passing the inconvenient proofs of material reality) transforms principle into dogma – not to mention going over students' heads, which is the problem of all systems of thought: they lose touch. Indeed, what has to be kept always in mind is the sense that theoretical activity is dependent upon and caught up in a historically oriented struggle with materially organized and ideologically constructed (produced) *orders of power.* And beyond this there is the fact that the process we are involved in is no mere intellectual game – that it is going on 'out there', at every level of social life; and that we all bring it into the classroom with us as our environment, since even the language we use is part of the praxis of living, of things happening, being lived and changed around us.

In other words, we have to make ourselves aware that this *is* a struggle, against attitudes, against verbal (and psychological) assumptions, in the attempt to open ourselves up to the underlying conditions, to the dialogic, dialectic possibilities of discourse, the conditions of active social practice, both in the immediate interchange of opinions in the class and in our response to whatever written text we may be dealing with. This suggests that (in the development of any argument) the Marxian analysis would need at the very least to take into account not only the material conditions at work upon us but also those energies and drives determined by psychological and sexual disposition – the psychoanalytical and feminist contexts. For no dialectic view of the interaction between individual and society as embodied in the complexities of the literary text can afford to ignore such complementary and essential issues.

So how should one proceed? First perhaps by affirming, with Raymond Williams (1977:211-12), that 'writing is always communication ... always in some sense self-communication and social composition', even as it is 'often a new articulation and in effect a new formulation'; and by refusing to separate writing as art from other aspects of social activity, since to do so would be 'to lose contact with the substantive creative process and then to idealize it' – to put it into a kind of sealed-off category labelled 'art'. And secondly by recognizing the terms under which the social contexts of self-composition (creative activity) set up a continuing (and creative) tension between the individual voice (as speaker, writer, reader) and the society it is a product of.

Let us now proceed by applying these methods to a particular text, and imagine taking that text in hand. Let us suppose we have been debating the nature of the theoretical process, as outlined above, and that the students are now coming into class to discuss Joseph Conrad's *Heart of Darkness* for the first of two weekly two-hour seminars. This indeed is the way it actually happened at the Polytechnic. The students were still only in the second semester of their first year. They had already completed an introductory module on the modernist movement, but they hadn't as yet got any sort of clear understanding of the Marxian dialectic. According to the records I have kept on one seminar-group of eight students, preliminary questions registered general agreement that the book offers a devastating critique of the impact on Africa of Western imperialism. But when questioned about the political-social context Conrad was responding to, no-one seemed to have anything more than a vague sense of the actual conditions or what the word 'imperialism' signified. So it was necessary first of all to give them some idea of the momentous changes that had been taking place in Europe in the thirty years preceding 1899, the year Conrad wrote *Heart of Darkness*: the Franco-Prussian War, Bismarck's plans for the unification of Germany, the Italian Risorgimento, the defeat of the Paris Commune, the ominous development of German industrial power, the new and staggering imperialist expansion of Europe into Africa and the Middle and Far East, the Bismarckian bid for hegemony of Europe: 'Deutschland über Alles' (see Hobsbawn 1987:142-3). But what concerned us above all, as it concerned Conrad, was the rapacious carving-up of Africa by the forces of European monopoly capitalism in the search for new world markets, and the scale of it. For this, I referred the students to Lenin's concentrated 1916 study *Imperialism: The Latest State of Capitalism*, which provides crucial and telling facts, demonstrating that, whereas in 1870 only one-tenth of Africa had been colonized, by 1900 only one-tenth remained *uncolonized*. Members of the seminar were asked to read the pamphlet (see Lenin 1982).

All this confirmed what the students had picked up from the book – the tone of shock, disgust and disillusion that runs through it, in the spirit, for instance, of Marlow's allusion, early on, to the colonialist enterprise:

> They grabbed what they could get for the sake of what was to be got. It was just robbery with violence, aggravated murder on a great scale, and men going at it blind – as is very proper for those who tackle a darkness. The conquest of the earth, which mostly means the taking it away from those who have a different complexion or slightly flatter noses than ourselves, is not a pretty thing when you look at it too much.
> (Conrad 1985:31-2; page references henceforth will be to this edition of *Heart of Darkness*)

Here, with what Fredric Jameson identifies as 'Conrad's unquestionable and acute sense of the nature and dynamics of imperialist penetration' (Jameson 1983:215), it seemed possible to argue the terms of the Marxist dialectic concerning the reality of materialist production as 'the foundation of the sensuous world' of human society (Marx and Engels 1976:46).

But what we had to tackle was the way the book develops. For this *apparent* awareness of history and of material existence, of 'the productive relationship of human beings to nature', is almost at once 'sytematically displaced' into myth – the 'mysterious life of the wilderness that stirs in the forest, in the jungle, in the hearts of wild men' (Jameson 1983:215). As Marlow tells us, 'there's no initiation ... into such mysteries' (31); and later: 'It is impossible to convey the life-sensation of any given epoch of one's existence – that which makes its truth, its meaning' (57). One is faced instead with 'the incomprehensible ... the fascination of the abomination' (31), an existential sense of 'the absurdity of human existence in the face of a *malevolent* Nature' (Jameson 1983:216), and the futility of the ordering norms of social reality.

In fact, the difficulties of the text *begin* with the problem of displacement (of psychic dislocation), which is inseparable from Conrad's ambiguous treatment of his theme. The author casts a kind of spell upon the reader from the start, launching into the narrative by means of a double device at once distancing and intimate. First he sets the scene on the Thames as one of a group of reflective listening presences; and then (almost before we are aware of it) merges this voice into the voice of Marlow – thus inducing in the reader an equivalent condition of attentive passivity. And from this point on it is Marlow's obsessive and increasingly mystifying rhetoric that takes over, dictating the tone, creating in us a state of appalled expectancy, *as nothing more than a voice*, coming at us like 'one of those misty haloes that sometimes are made visible by the spectral illumination of moonshine' (30).

The task of the reader as critic – and the task of the students in the seminar – is then to step back from the fictive web being woven by the storyteller and attempt to make visible the hidden (or displaced) ideological assumptions of the text, to bring them to the surface and identify them in terms of the social and historical realities Marlow insistently and symptomatically blurs over. There is, for instance, the generalising nature of the imagery, which blends all rivers and seas into one another and all mankind into an a-historical condition, an 'inherent solidarity' (8), which undermines difference and particularity. There is Marlow's Congo – isolated, primitive, undefinable, no longer the much-used waterway organized to accommodate the constant traffic of the traders, as Conrad himself had known it – turned into a setting for a mythical journey into the self in search of the 'truth'. For him, 'going up the river was like going back to the earliest beginnings of the world, when ... the big trees were kings' (66) or 'travelling in the night of first ages, of those ages that are gone', where 'the mind of man is capable of anything – because everything is in it, all the past as well as all the future' (69). And it is *there* you find truth. Beyond the 'surface reality', all the attention paid to details of sensation and of action, is the 'inner meaning'. In other words, it is *Marlow's* experience of the journey that matters – what is going on inside *him, his* struggle to resist the wilderness – rather than any sort of objective recognition, any real sense of the historical-social presence of Africa. For him, beyond the detail ('Let the fool gape and shudder – the man knows'), is 'truth stripped of its cloak of time' (69).

'But what is this truth?' we had to ask. 'What does it reveal?' In its blurring of distinctions between the surface reality and the inner reality, we are increasingly encouraged to associate it with the madness of Kurtz, the surrender of the 'soul' to darkness, a yielding up of all sense of restraint and of substance to the domination of a compulsive voice. And in dealing with these questions, what we had to wrestle with was the extent to which this revelation of a soul gone mad provides accusatory proofs of the nightmare consequences of Europe's racist exploitation of Africa. For it comes at us distorted, with 'the terrific suggestiveness of words heard in dreams, of phrases spoken in nightmares' (108); of someone 'being assaulted by the powers of darkness' (85). So it seems that in Kurtz 'both the diabolic love and the unearthly hate of the mysteries it had penetrated fought for possession of that soul' (110), leaving it at the end in a state of 'intense and hopeless despair', in 'an impenetrable darkness' (111), with Marlow witnessing the struggle, and wanting only to to lay the ghost of Kurtz's 'gifts', to put it to 'everlasting rest in the dust-bin of progress, amongst all the sweepings and, figuratively speaking, all the dead cats of civilization' (87).

The bitterness – 'so withering to one's belief in mankind' (108) – is palpable. And behind it, reflecting an existential uncertainty endemic to the forms of bourgeois culture at the time, is the hidden voice of the author, dictating the narrative, actively displacing history, insisting that there are metaphysical, moral forces at work, mysteries not to be fathomed, which bring Marlow up against a substanceless and indescribable evil, a spiritual blankness at the centre of existence.

In these terms history vanishes – as much the history of the Congo and its people as that of those who are assumed to have 'solid pavement' (85) under their feet. And what we are left with is the metaphysics of the self, trapped in an impenetrable darkness, 'the stillness of an implacable force brooding over an inscrutable intention' (66), which a plethora of adjectives expressing bafflement and horror serves increasingly to emphasize. Author and reader are drawn deeper into an unanswerable (and incomprehensible) enigma – which, in spite of the subjective immediacy of the narrative, remains shadowy, tenuous, indefinite, undefinable, unspeakable; history absorbed into myth.

Discussing such issues as these in the seminar-group – tentatively at the first meeting and in more depth at the second – became in effect a debate about the impact of the book, the ways in which its cumulative momentum, driven by a bleak pessimism, carries the reader deeper and deeper into a disorientating world of psychic disorder. This brought us to ask what Conrad's systematic displacement of the historical-material process actually signifies in the terms of Marlow's mythical 'night of first ages', where principles are mere 'rags that would fly off at the first good shake' (69), and ordinary people, 'so full of stupid importance', dreaming 'their insignificant and silly dreams' (113), vanish (like the people of Africa) into the shadows. And these questions led finally (and briefly) to an attempt to place Conrad's modernism, its internalizing aesthetics, its subjective and a-historical vision of reality, in the context of the 'objective pre-conditions' of capitalism – that 'increasing fragmentation both of the rationalized external world and of the colonized psyche alike' (Jameson 1983:236) – which characterized the modernist movement at the turn of the century.

The seminars did not reach any final conclusions about the book. We had simply established ways of setting it against the historical contradictions of the world in which it was written, both as an indictment of imperialism and as a reaction to and a symptom of the dislocating process of monopoly capitalism at work. And the problems it raised – of ideology, of representation, of history, of cultural production – now had to be addressed again in terms of the interactive conditions of the Marxian dialectic and its refusal to permit the underlying forms of material production to be left out of the argument.

But at the same time, such problems – and particularly that which defines literary activity as an ideological product – could now be pursued in the parallel course of *Renaissance Poetry and Drama*, and applied to the texts being studied there – Marlowe's *Faustus*, Jonson's *Volpone*, Shakespeare's *Measure for Measure*, written at a time when England was undergoing radical transformation, with the feudal system breaking down and the forces of competitive individualism beginning to take over.

This was, in other words, an ongoing, difficult and complex process – an investigation of the underlying conditions of cultural production and of the ideological conventions set up to justify and confirm them. And if it can be agreed that literature constitutes 'an influential medium through which certain ways of thinking about the world are promoted and others impeded', then it is the teacher's (and the student-critic's) task to open up this medium to *radical questioning*, and to make texts 'a site of cultural struggle and change' (Sinfield 1985:131).

Literary Hermeneutics and Pedagogics after Deconstruction: The Rationalist-Historicist Alternative

Per Serritslev Petersen, University of Aarhus, Denmark

Let me make clear from the outset that the main argument of this paper will be based on the presupposition that literary hermeneutics, as the science or art of *interpreting* literature, and literary pedagogics, as the science or art of *teaching* literature, should be dialectically implicated in one another. In other words, literary theory – and the teaching of literary theory – should have a direct and directive bearing on the way we actually analyse and interpret literary texts: not Theory for Theory's sake (the current fad in the more progressive literary academies of the Western hemisphere, which to me spells theory fetishism and solipsism), but theory as a form of methodological and epistemological underpinning of literary studies as these happen to be organized and practised within a given English-department curriculum (say, in terms of core courses on British and American literary history). Let me also confess straightaway (now that I have struck a confessional note) that my own literary hermeneutics has always been biased towards historicism; indeed, I seem to be a congenital historicist, a literary historian philosophically affiliated with what Jacques Derrida would term Western logocentric metaphysics – the kind of interpreter that, in the well-known words of Derrida's 'Structure, Sign and Play in the Discourse of the Human Sciences' (1966), 'seeks to decipher, dreams of deciphering a truth or an origin which escapes play, and [who] lives the necessity of interpretation as an exile' (Lodge 1988:121-22). I believe there are at least two good reasons for this pathetic clinging to the old Enlightenment metaphysics: first, 'I gotta use words when I talk to you', as T.S. Eliot's Sweeney Agonistes put it (Eliot 1963:135), and even Derrida has to admit that 'we have no language – no syntax and no lexicon – which is foreign to [the history of Western metaphysics]' (Lodge 1988:111); second, I'm not particularly keen on Derrida's joyous and playful Nietzschean metaphysics, his poststructuralist and posthumanist 'monstrosity' (Lodge 1988:122) – I am not, of course, alluding here to his late deconstructionist friend Paul de Man's version of 'monstrous' metaphysics and politics, past and present.

In my student days, back in the 1960s, literary theory – still invisible in the curricular landscape of English studies then – meant *Theory of Literature* (1942), that is, New Criticism according to Wellek and Warren. I still recall my acute sense of frustration and mystification when I first read about the paradoxical nature of the literary work of art: timeless and historical at the same time, possessing a substantial identity of structure, but also highly dynamic, 'passing through the minds of readers, critics, and fellow artists' (Wellek and Warren 1956:144). Still, I was told not to worry too much about the messy hermeneutical implications of this 'dynamic' antihistoricism, that is, the danger of 'mere subjectivism and relativism':

> It will always be possible to determine which point of view grasps the subject most thoroughly and deeply. A hierarchy of viewpoints, a criticism of the grasp of norms, is implied in the concept of the adequacy of interpretation. All relativism is ultimately defeated by the recognition that 'the Absolute is in the relative, though not finally and fully in it'.
>
> (Wellek and Warren 1956:144)

Needless to say, this highfalutin twaddle made my still innocent hermeneutical soul even more worried – and baffled too: was I really supposed to take such obscurantism seriously? Eventually I decided I wasn't, and I launched what I then – and still today – would like to conceive of as my rationalist and historicist project in literary hermeneutics (see, for instance, Petersen 1980).

Interdisciplinarity became an integral part of that project. Thus the question of scientific rationality – there simply had to be a more rationalist alternative to Wellek and Warren's New-Critical obscurantism – necessitated a closer look at humanistic studies in a broader philosophy-of-science perspective. In his little book *The Semantics of Literature* (1966), Trevor Eaton had noted that literature was 'one of the few disciplines which had withstood the onslaught of the scientific method', and, as he regarded 'the university as a depository of knowledge on any given subject', he would 'expect to find a progression in knowledge in the study of literature in the same sense in which this can be seen in scientific subjects' (Eaton 1966:10, 60). Ten years later E.D. Hirsch made a similar point in *The Aims of Interpretation* (1976) when he pronounced literary study to be 'at present the most skeptical and decadent branch of humanistic study', and, as one of the more important causes of the malaise, he singled out 'its anxiety-ridden insistence, more emphatic than in any other field, on distinguishing itself from natural science' (Hirsch 1976:149). Exactitude of knowledge is a variable in all scientific fields, and 'despite the century-old distinction between humanistic and scientific enquiry, the cognitive elements in both have exactly the same character' (Hirsch 1976:149). I naturally agreed with both Eaton and Hirsch on this issue, as I also concurred with the conclusion reached by Roy Bhaskar in *The Possibility of Naturalism: A Philosophical Critique of the Contemporary Human Sciences* (1979), viz. that 'the human sciences can be sciences *in exactly the same sense*, though *not in exactly the same way*, as the natural ones' (Bhaskar 1979:203).

Karl Popper turned out to be the philosopher of science that I found most congenial to my ongoing project, that is, my attempt to outline the methodological foundation of a literary hermeneutics on rationalist and historicist principles. But first I should mention another interdisciplinary dimension of the project, which I also found it necessary to explore, and which is – or, at least, ought to be – somewhat closer to home, viz. linguistics, language study as traditionally distinct from literary study. Wellek and Warren had, in point of fact, raised 'the question of historical "reconstructionism", its possibility and desirability' (Wellek and Warren 1956:167), but this question had, predictably, been given very short shrift (less than half a page), the whole issue being a non-starter in the radically antihistoricist hermeneutics of New Criticism. In my project, however, historical reconstruction and contextualization would naturally be deemed a methodological *sine qua non*. As Roger D. Sell has recently stressed in his introduction to *Literary Pragmatics* (1991), the writing and reading of literary texts should be seen as 'interactive communication processes', and, like all such processes, 'inextricably linked with the particular sociocultural contexts within which they take place' (Sell 1991:xiv); 'literary works, far from being airless aesthetic heterocosms, are complexly consubstantial with ongoing processes of discourse in society as a whole' (xxi). And the interdisciplinary Literary Pragmatics Project at Åbo Akademi University was, Sell points out, based on the belief that the emphasis on contextualization could also open up dialogues between linguists and literary scholars (xiii). A reasonable belief, to be sure. As regards the rationality of my own literary-hermeneutics project, it was precisely the methodological relevance of contextualization – be it historical, cultural, ideological, literary or linguistic – that made me turn to the sociolinguistics and sociosemantics of M.A.K. Halliday: the concept of meaning potential as 'a network of socio-semantic options' (Halliday 1973:65), interpretation conceptualized as 'a positive act of semiotic reconstruction' (Halliday 1975:140), etc. And through Halliday I would finally arrive at the doorstep of J.R. Firth, the founding father of contextualist semantics, who, in his early essay 'The Technique of Semantics' (1935), memorably described interpretation as 'a serial contextualization of our facts, context within context, each one being a function, an organ of the bigger context, and all contexts finding a place in what may be called the context of culture' (Firth 1957:32).

At this stage, the project was ready for Karl Popper and his philosophy of science. In his essay 'On the Theory of the Objective Mind' – chapter 4 of *Objective Knowledge* (1972) – Popper deals with the problem of historical understanding, and his thesis is briefly that 'the main aim of all historical understanding is the hypothetical reconstruction of a historical *problem-situation*' (Popper 1972:170). This thesis is fleshed out, as it were, by a hermeneutical method which Popper calls situational logic or situational analysis, and which he describes as follows:

> By situational analysis I mean a certain kind of tentative or conjectural explanation of some human action which appeals to the situation in which the agent finds himself. It may be a historical explanation: we may perhaps wish to explain how and why a certain structure of ideas was created. Admittedly, no creative action can ever be fully explained. Nevertheless, we can try, conjecturally, to give an idealized reconstruction of the *problem situation* in which the agent found himself, and to that extent make the action 'understandable' (or 'rationally understandable'), that is to say, *adequate to his situation as he saw it*. This method of situational analysis may be described as an application of the *rationality principle*. (Popper 1972:179)

The hermeneutical method of situational analysis, which can be seen to fit in nicely with the contextualization model of sociolinguistics (and anthropological linguistics), could then, I thought, be combined with Popper's general schema of scientific problem-solving, that is, 'the method of imaginative conjectures and criticism' or simply 'the method of conjecture and refutation' (Popper 1972:164). The method is graphically represented as follows:

$$P_1 \rightarrow TT \rightarrow EE \rightarrow P_2$$

The schema, which I have gratefully appropriated for my literary hermeneutics, is explained as follows:

> P_1 is the *problem* from which we start, *TT* (the 'the tentative theory') is the imaginative conjectural solution which we first reach, for example our first *tentative interpretation*. *EE* ('*error elimination*') consists of severe critical examination of our conjecture, our tentative interpretation: it consists, for example, of the critical use of documentary evidence and, if we have at this early stage more than one conjecture at our disposal, it will also consist of a critical discussion and comparative evaluation of the competing conjectures. P_2 is the problem situation as it emerges from our first critical attempt to solve our problems. It leads up to our second attempt (*and so on*). (Popper 1972:164)

I have no qualms about this appropriation from Popper's philosophy of science because I don't see why there should be any *essential* difference between a literary scholar's quest for the meaning of, say, Wordsworth's Lucy poem 'A Slumber Did My Spirit Seal' and an Einstein's quest for 'the perfect rule of law within a world of some objective reality which [he was trying] to catch in a wildly speculative way' (the famous statement made by Einstein in a letter to Max Born). The scientific method of problem-solving, the method of imaginative conjecture and critical refutation, could, in principle, be practised by humanist and scientist alike, so, in Popper's phrase, 'labouring the difference between science and the humanities has long been a fashion, and has become a bore' (Popper 1972:185).

So much for the philosophy and methodology of my literary hermeneutics, but the next and crucial question is of course: how does all this impinge upon literary pedagogics, the theory and practice of teaching literature (my initial postulate being that hermeneutics and pedagogics should somehow be dialectically implicated in one another)? Well, first I had better briefly review the curricular set-up within which the literary studies of my department are currently organized. In the two-year basic-studies programme, the literary set-up may be defined as a tripartite structure comprising (a) a two-semester humanistic philosophy-of-science course (mainly literary theory, but also some linguistic and cultural theory); (b) a three-semester literary-history course (British, American, and Commonwealth literatures); (c) 1-3 one-semester topic seminars (in-depth studies of particular authors, periods, genres, themes etc). The literary 'core course' is obviously the literary-history course, the objectives of which are, to quote the official study and exam regulations (1991), to give the student (a) 'basic knowledge about the literatures in English, that is, British, American and some Commonwealth literatures'; and (b) 'ability to systematically analyse and interpret given texts in their relevant literary-history, cultural-history and social-history contexts'. Thus, as far as the official curricular policy is concerned, there can hardly be any doubt about the historicist orientation of the literary-studies programme. But then, of course, policy is one thing, actual practice another, and there is literary history and literary history, all depending on which teachers happen to teach the course (my present colleagues span the entire theoretical spectrum from Marxism/Culturalism to New Criticism/Deconstructionism).

Under these circumstances, in the prevailing departmental state of methodological pluralism or anarchism (some of the theories professed and taught being clearly incommensurable), the proposition of teaching literary theory (in the philosophy-of-science course) with a direct and directive bearing on the practical study of literary texts (in the literary-history course and the topic seminars) is doomed to failure. Theoretical conversions or paradigm shifts don't happen overnight, if at all, and humanists, literary scholars in particular, are inveterate individualists: joint research programmes based on some heuristic *hard core* '"irrefutable" by the methodological decision of its protagonists' (Latakos 1972:133) are the exceptions that prove the rule in the humanities. So, by and large, the individual teacher and scholar is left to his own hermeneutical and pedagogical devices. Teaching a literary-theory course (typically, twentieth-century theories from Russian Formalism to Deconstructionism) as it is supposed to be taught today, that is, without any clear pragmatic (curricular) sense of a means-to-an-end instrumentality, can prove a pretty harrowing exercise in pluralistic tolerance (for a discussion of the pragmatism/theoreticism issue in the curricular designing of literary studies, see Petersen forthcoming). Even the late Raman Selden, the doyen of contemporary Anglo-Saxon literary theory, after successfully persuading himself that 'it may seem best to say "let many flowers bloom" and to treat the plenitude of theories as a cornucopia to be enjoyed and tasted with relish' (Selden 1989:7), would have to admit that, at a certain stage, 'students will want to know which tradition [or theory] has the best claim to truth, validity, relevance, or explanatory power' (5). Now 'how much claim to hermeneutical truth, validity, relevance, or explanatory power' – one could very well imagine a mentally 'deconstructed' student asking – 'did Derrida's essay "Structure, Sign and Play in the Discourses of the Human Sciences" actually have? After all, we spent three hours discussing the essay before we could even begin to have any idea about what the *theory*, if any, was all about. Was it really worth our while as students of English literature?'

However, before the student could start asking that kind of question, he must, of course, have some rough idea of what it means, or could mean, to be a student of English literature. So it is not a question of whether literary theory should be taught – it should: after New Criticism, literary studies sorely needed a dose of theoreticism. It is a question of what kind of literary theory it makes sense to teach within a given curricular set-up. When I was last asked to teach literary theory (the Russian-Formalism-to-Deconstructionism type of course), two of the objectives I announced in my course programme were the following:

– engaging theoretical and philosophical issues that are inevitably raised by – and, consequently, can be recognized as being relevant to – the way we read, study and interpret literary texts (thus the launching pad of the course will be a discussion of a specific interpretative problem, viz. the meaning of Wordsworth's poem 'A Slumber Did My Spirit Seal')

– encouraging you to make up your own minds in this highly contentious field of debate, and if some of you should protest that literary theory – theorizing about how to read literature – 'gets in the way between the reader and the work', then my response would be the same as Terry Eagleton's, viz. that 'without some kind of theory, however unreflective and implicit, we would not know what a "literary work" was in the first place, or how we were to read it' [Eagleton 1983:viii]

Pedagogically, it is of paramount importance that it is the student – and not the teacher – that first identifies and ponders the 'theoretical and philosophical issues' that constitute the subject matter of literary theory as an academic discipline. My 'launching pad' was intended to expose the student, from the very start, to the nitty-gritty of hermeneutical practice: how to cope with a specific interpretative problem, complete with six divergent or contradictory solutions, viz. 'expert' readings by six literary critics and scholars: Cleanth Brooks, F.W. Bateson, Margaret Drabble, David B. Pirie, Geoffrey H. Hartmann, and Paul de Man. Brooks's and Bateson's interpretations were accompanied by E.D. Hirsch's commentary in *Validity in Interpretation*

(Hirsch 1967:227-32), seeing that one of the crucial issues to be debated in class would be the question whether it makes sense at all to talk about valid or correct interpretations in literary studies. The students were simply asked to select their favourite readings and motivate their choice. Besides this, they were asked to study a selection of what I termed Wordsworth con-texts (the other Lucy poems, 'Expostulation and Reply', 'The Tables Turned', stanza 5 of the Immortality Ode, and a few extracts from 'Tintern Abbey' and *The Prelude*). In the class discussion they had no problem in identifying the more blatantly contradictory interpretations, and by analysing the reasons the students gave for their individual preferences, we fairly quickly reached the 'programmed' theoretical bottom line: historicism vs. antihistoricism; Bateson, Drabble, Pirie and Hartmann vs. Brooks and de Man; various versions of historicist hermeneutics vs. antihistoricist New Criticism and Deconstructionism. Most of the students (but not all) found the historicist-contextualist interpretation of Lucy's sublime cosmic epitaph, magnificently encoded in Wordsworth's romantic pastoralism, pantheism and primitivism, more stimulating and exciting than Brooks's and de Man's modern(ist), tragic-ironic readings: Lucy's 'utter and horrible inertness', 'falling back into the clutter of things', 'touched by and held by earthly time in its most powerful and horrible image' (Brooks 1962:736); 'first there was error, then the death occurred, and now an internal insight into the rocky barrenness of the human condition prevails' (de Man 1971:225) – the latter (mis)reading being a curiously naive instance of what Frank Lentricchia, in his essay 'Paul de Man: The Rhetoric of Authority', has characterized as 'the formalist's final response to a repressed and alienated social existence' (Lentricchia 1983:317).

The issue of historicism vs. antihistoricism was rounded off by a brief discussion of E.D. Hirsch's bottom-line distinction, in 'The Politics of Theories of Interpretation' (1982), between the autocratic and allocratic norm in hermeneutics, the antihistoricist 'reader-norm' and the historicist 'author-norm': 'Under the autocratic norm, authority resides in the reader, while under the allocratic norm, the reader delegates authority to the reconstructed historical act of another person or community' (Hirsch 1987:176). Here the question of theory and all that dry-as-dust reconstruction and contextualization 'getting in between the reader and the work' cropped up once more, and we then discussed the different kinds of reading we perform in our daily lives, from con-amore bedtime readings of favourite authors and genres to studying *Macbeth* complete with critical introduction, footnotes and casebooks in the library. And the point we ended up debating, in a reasonably constructive spirit, was whether con-amore readings and more academic readings would invariably and necessarily be radically distinct exercises: if you were reading, say, *American Psycho* con amore, you would probably, consciously as well as unconsciously, be drawing not only on your own experiential background, but also on your more specific knowledge about contemporary American culture, the New York/Wall Street culture of the yuppie-narcissistic 1980s in particular, and, if you happened to have read, say, Tom Wolfe's *The Bonfire of the Vanities* in the not too distant past (or seen the film version – and, perhaps, also recent American films within or close to the horror-and-splatter genre, say, *The Silence of the Lambs*), you would find it very hard not to do a bit of con-amore contextualizing on your own. So there really needn't be any *essential* difference, I would plead, between the 'informed' con-amore reading outside the classroom and the academic study inside. In both cases, we would be dealing with (and I might now be tempted to paraphrase Sell in the introduction to *Literary Pragmatics)* specific interactive communication processes, inextricably linked with the particular sociocultural contexts within which they take place.

My literary-theory students would be spared, though, a fully-fledged lecture on my own literary hermeneutics on rationalist and historicist principles - unless they explicitly asked for it. Now, this 'asking-for-it' might typically happen in a topic seminar (where there would be no acute problem of 'theory glut', but a more pedagogically balanced theory/practice dialectic), as it actually did happen in one of the seminars I am teaching at present, viz. a seminar on 'Comedy and Politics from Shakespeare to Congreve'. Apart from a variety of 'con-texts' on the theatrical, ideological, political and socio-economic background, the seminar bibliography comprised the following comedies: Shakespeare's *The Merchant of Venice* (1596) and *Twelfth Night* (1601), Jonson's *Volpone* (1606), Massinger's *The City Madam* (1632), Wycherley's *The Country Wife* (1675), Etherege's *The Man of Mode* (1676), and Congreve's *Love for Love* (1695). In my seminar programme the main theme or objective was defined as follows:

> In this seminar we shall trace the development of English comedy in the century of revolution, and we shall see how the transformations of English comedy from Shakespeare's *Merchant of Venice* (1596) to Congreve's *Love for Love* (1695) reflected or mediated, satirically and otherwise, the transformations outside the theatre – constitutional, political, etc.

As far as the Shakespeare, Jonson, and Massinger plays were concerned, the comedy-and-politics approach was mainly focused on the ways in which a politically disruptive socioeconomic tension in Elizabethan/Jacobean/Carolean society was ideologically manipulated and contained through displacement within the generic conventions of comedy. In *The Merchant of Venice* and *The City Madam*, for instance, the problematic 'real-life' moneyman, that is, the acquisitive bourgeois moneylender who threatens the welfare and status of some needy aristocratic client (represented, in the comedies, by Bassanio and Lord Lacy), is first displaced through what I dubbed a doubling or DrJekyll/-MrHyde gimmick: good (too-good-to-be-true Christian) Antonio vs. evil (demoniacally Jewish) Shylock; the good (within reason) merchant Sir John

Frugal vs. the evil (hypocritical and atheistical) brother Luke. Next, the evil moneymen are opportunely cast as villains in their respective comedies and thus come to an appropriately sticky end. Likewise, the 'real' socioeconomic issue is glossed over, as it were, through ideological displacement: in Shakespeare's comedy it becomes a simple or simplistic question of choosing between Christian/aristocratic generosity and Jewish/puritanical monstrosity; in Massinger's play the question of *social* decorum (the proper 'distance 'twixt the city and the court') is further submerged by the question of *sexual* decorum (if the city madams and their daughters could only be taught to behave themselves and pay due respect to the distance between female and male as well as city and the court ...).

The students were asked to prepare 'discussion agendas' for each play, that is, select and present four or five questions within the comedy-and-politics framework which they would like to discuss in class. Due to the amount of initial 'con-text' reading and the hermeneutical complexity of the historical re-construction/contextualization procedure (as compared to, say, a New-Critical approach) it took a couple of weeks before the level of student participation was satisfactory. After another couple of weeks some of the students had really got 'turned on' and could have run the show or seminar on their own – and possibly run away with it. Anyway, the level of student participation at this stage now made me pleasantly aware of the need somehow to balance pedagogically between 'teacherly' or 'masterminding' control and the (from the teacher's point of view at least) potential anarchy of 'hyperactive' student participation. It is worth noticing, I think, that the more articulate and dynamic students had, as a rule, been working and discussing together, prior to the class, in study groups (3-5 students per group), which had been organized at the beginning of the seminar (but as an option only). I should also mention, perhaps, that my ERASMUS students from Britain commented explicitly on the 'Danish' or 'Continental' style of hermeneutics and pedagogics, both the 'context' orientation (at home, 'context' was still considered taboo in some places, they claimed), and the fact that such matters could be debated in the classroom here.

What triggered off the full-scale discussion of historicist as opposed to antihistoricist hermeneutics in the seminar was *The Man of Mode*, particularly the libertine rake-hero of the comedy. The students had been asked to study Robert D. Hume's discussion of the play, especially what Hume claims to be the 'basic issue' and 'nasty question' of *The Man of Mode*, viz. 'is Dorimant meant to be admired?' (Hume 1976:86-87). Hume doesn't come up with any clear answers, but he does suggest that 'presumably [*sic*] the Carolean audience applied its own standards, and [that] these may differ from ours' (89). Most of the students were now prepared to argue (some of them pretty volubly) that if you had ordered your hermeneutical priorities, opted for historicism, and done your reconstruction/contextualization homework (that is, related the character of Dorimant to hermeneutically relevant contexts like Hobbesian naturalism, Carolean libertinism, the 'sociology' of Restoration theatre, etc.), the question wouldn't be that nasty. Indeed, you would have to agree with John Dennis's statement, in 'A Defence of Sir Fopling Flutter' (1722), that Dorimant was meant to be an 'admirable Picture of a Courtier in the Court of King *Charles* the Second', and that otherwise the portrait would not have been accepted or appreciated by the original audience (according to Dennis, Dorimant was considered to be modelled on Lord Rochester).

There is no doubt that some of my students would still insist that all this historicist theorization and contextualization 'gets in between the reader and the work'. This presents a pedagogical problem which I frankly can't solve in *my* classroom. One obvious reason why Derridean Deconstruction has had such a vogue in the US is surely, as Bernard Bergonzi observes in *Exploding English* (1990), that it 'provided a convenient successor to the New Criticism in mass higher education, providing a form of detailed close analysis of texts which does not require much in the way of contextual cultural theory' (Bergonzi 1990:131). However, pedagogical opportunism as an argument for Deconstruction is unacceptable if you believe, as I do, (a) that hermeneutics and pedagogics should be dialectically implicated in one another; and (b) that hermeneutics deserves to be taken very seriously as an academic and humanistic discipline in today's world. As Robert Scholes points out in *Textual Power: Literary Theory and the Teaching of English* (1985), the students that come to us now exist in the most manipulative culture human beings have ever experienced: 'They are bombarded with signs, with rhetoric, from their daily awakenings until their troubled sleep, especially with signs transmitted by the audio-visual media' (Scholes 1985:15). A literary hermeneutics on rationalist and historicist principles could, apart from constituting the methodology of a literary-history study programme, also offer the student a vital cognitive instrument with which to encounter the bombardment of the manipulative culture outside the classroom. On that issue I can whole-heartedly endorse both the politics and the hermeneutics/pedagogics of Scholes's conception of 'textual power':

> what [the students] need from us now is the kind of knowledge and skill that will enable them to make sense of their worlds, to determine their own interests, both individual and collective, to see through the manipulations of all sorts of texts in all sorts of media, and to express their own views in some appropriate manner. That they need both knowledge and skill is perhaps a matter worth pausing to consider. We have sometimes behaved as if certain skills, such as composition and even the close reading of poems, could be developed apart from knowledge, especially apart from historical knowledge. We are paying the price for that error now. One does not have to be a Marxist to endorse Fredric Jameson's battle cry, 'Always historicize!' (the first words of *The Political Unconscious*).
> (Scholes 1985:15-16)

What Does 'English' Do? Thoughts on Rewriting

Robert Clark, University of East Anglia, UK

The 1980s were years of revenge. The 1960s ethos of idealistic collectivism has been replaced by what Mrs Thatcher called 'a return to Victorian values': hard work, money-making, self-interested acquisition. Actually this decoction of Adam Smith and Jeremy Bentham was not Victorian but desperately ultra-modern in its short-sighted individualism, and timelessly capitalist in its promotion of the individual and money-values. In Britain, one effect of this fundamental change of ethos on the teaching of literature was that we were encouraged and bullied into examining the vocational usefulness of a literary education. Despite the Monetarist declaration that the free market would be the arbiter of destiny from now on, it was no longer enough that nationally there were seven applicants for every place to read English at British universities, and for some programmes twenty to fifty. And it was no longer axiomatic that the development of the national culture was a necessary or good thing. Our Government considered most social sciences subversive, and most cultural activities 'wet'. University funding for the humanities was cut. Our future in jeopardy, we had to adopt a promotional jargon about the values of English. We learnt to boast of our students' 'transferable skills' and to argue that their 'learning outcomes' are 'enhanced communicative and analytic skills, the ability to work creatively and constructively in groups', and so on.

This attention to skills brought some benefits. As a young teacher in the late 1970s I remember being struck by the cultivated disconnectedness of life in an English Department. Students did not wish to consider what they would do after university, and the faculty, despite often critiquing Arnold and Eliot, saw themselves as addressing a critical elite (envisioned by the centre-right as 'disinterested' and by the centre-left as 'radical'), who were formed just like themselves and would never have to sully their hands with industry or commerce. Given that even in those halcyon days only 20% of our students went into teaching or research, this seemed head-in-the-sandish. But to point out that not all our students obtained firsts and became scholars, and to promote vacation placements with publishers as I then did, was looked at askance, even in a School which has a reputation for its interest in creative writing. During one Planning Meeting a colleague pointedly remarked that it was not the task of a university lecturer to concern himself with his students' careers.

The hostility to the humanities of Thatcherite conservatives changed this. It is now no longer shocking to ask what skills students learn during three years studying English. However, it is probable that this question is rarely asked with any desire to know the truth. Our basic institutional and personal desire is to carry on being just like ourselves, and most of the answers which come quick to the tongue would either be valid for any humanities course (the development of personal skills, for example), or be highly debatable (growth in humane understanding), so the question what is actually learned by studying a national literature is not satisfactorily answered. If one came from Mars and asked 'What does it mean, "to graduate in English?",' what kind of answer could one give?

Reading this year's examination scripts and asking myself 'What can they do? What do they know?' I have to confess my conclusions were rather dispiriting. As an initial clarification it seemed to me we could divide the possible skills and knowledges into three areas: knowledge of past and present literary texts, hermeneutic skills and expressive skills. This tripartite division could be otherwise expressed as: facts, analytic and theoretical procedures, rhetoric. A convincing general argument to our visitor from Mars might be that the study of these aspects of linguistic representations heightens the awareness of what has been and can be done in language, encourages an informed historical sense, develops the ability to see the world through the words of others (the liberal humanist argument), and to critique/unmask the strategies of representation (the radical political argument). Mastering these skills has a reflexive effect on students' own rhetorical skills and empowers them either to persuade in the name of politics or commerce, aid efficient administration, or critically defend 'the truth' against ideological misdirection.

I suspect that this thoroughly Enlightenment assertion constitutes the implicit ground of most literary study in universities today. But I wonder how well it stands up to practical and philosophical analysis. Given that most universities (even Oxford) now operate a modular selective course, one cannot say students know 'the tradition' or the fundamentals of any major genre, or the history of theory, or even a range of modern theories. They might know any or all of these things in some detail, but one cannot say, as one could of a scientist, that they all necessarily know the fundamentals of x, y or z. Their sense of historical evolution has been attenuated by valuable intellectual critiques of 'history,' 'evolution' and 'tradition'; and fragmented by the growth of special-topic teaching, a consequence of the specialisation of the publishing market and academic career structures. The liberal-humanist conviction about seeing the other person's point of view has been undermined by theoretical developments which firstly attacked the presumptions of humanism and empathy, and then placed our trust in the metatextual authority of theories that now stand between, or sometimes in place of, the old-fashioned triad of author-text-reader. It follows from this that the idea of the critic as ideological unmasker has also been attenuated, since now that it is no longer possible to believe in history or the individual (officially, at least), the activity of political critique has lost the co-ordinates that gave it point and value.

Personally, I have learned greatly from the critical debates of the last twenty years, and yet, since I see rocks all around and no other maps to steer by, I cling to the old-fashioned beliefs. Benighted I may be, but not alone. Where our undergraduates are concerned, however, I feel Deconstruction to be dominant, not that they deeply understand or engage with Deconstructionist philosophy, but rather that they are able to live in disconnected knowledges, and have no belief in, or concern to find, a grand metanarrative which connects them.

In sum, if 'to graduate in English' today does not seem to imply a specific kind of factual or theoretical knowledge, no more does it imply a particular conviction about the course of history, or the role of human understanding and human imagination within it. What then does it imply? Perhaps one can only say that it implies an ability to write a particular kind of text. Specimens of the genre must be recognised as relatively alike, because they are comparable for assessment, and relatively unsystematic in comparison with scientific texts, since they are perceived as expressive of the writer's individuality. The deeper ground of identity between these texts is harder to establish. They evidence a hermeneutic process that 'makes sense' of a (literary) text by discussing aspects of its content, form and context. The writer may address one or more such aspects, may articulate a coherent theory or proceed pragmatically, and may be a formalist entirely ignorant of context, or a contextualist entirely ignorant of form, or, which is more common, be vaguely somewhere in between. In fact, most essays of the genre 'undergraduate English essay' are logically, theoretically and historically loose, as indeed are most essays by their teachers. The tradition to which they belong goes back at least as far as the *essai* of Montaigne, in which, originally, one person tries (*essays*) to make sense of an aspect of experience. However, the personal experimental character of the *essai* tends to be submerged by the search for other forms of security in modern writers, usually science, theory or philosophy. Students tend to write about a text as if writing about the world from the position of one who appears to know volumes, and in fact knows life mainly through a little literature. However 'good' such a text is when judged by the university assessment criteria, the effectiveness of students as literary critics depends to a degree on their ability to pretend to deep social convictions and kinds of historical knowledge, the first of which can rarely have been tested by experience, and the second of which is usually impossible without a lifetime of work. The characteristic of the university-undergraduate literary essay genre is, in effect, an immature imitation of the authoritative discourse of the parental generation. If the imitation is highly competent and a little transgressive, it is seen as a healthy reinvigoration, and labelled 'first-class quality'. If it is essentially a highly or partially competent repetition, it is classed in the UK as a second, upper or lower.

This process of imitation is not inherently bad. Indeed, what is most education but an apprenticeship for adult life through learning the codes, a mastering of disciplines and being mastered by them? But although most colleagues would agree to this description in the abstract, in practice, say in the examiners' meeting, the fact that we are approving repetitions and rewritings is concealed by the rhetoric of 'intelligence', 'intellect', 'originality', 'sensitivity' – valuations internal to a genre whose social role and value are taken for granted. However, the reporter from Mars might ask whether the production of this combination of analytic and hermeneutic skills, and the ranking of our students from first to third in accordance with their ability to reproduce it, is actually the most beneficial educational experience for our students, or for society, and whether it deserves the certification of a 'graduate in English Literature'.

Since reporters from outer space always behave like humanoids, we can be sure our hypothetical visitor would recognise, with all known human societies, the need to charge an intellectual class with the custodianship and reinterpretation of those texts which have sacral-sacred functions in the body politic. If Martian society has had a philosophical Enlightenment and undergone capitalist development, she will also take it as fundamentally important to the maintenance of democracy and the improvement-dynamic of history that this class acts not merely as curator but as critic, sounding out new paths for new times. She might then find it rather perturbing that support for this class has not recently been evident in the halls of British government, besotted as they have been by the myopic utilitarian capitalism of the Monetarist school. Equally, she might find it odd that the Left has rather undermined the second justification through its critique of 'the tradition' and the idea of 'literature' itself. If nothing's sacred, you don't need priests.

Her brain teased by disagreements Left and Right, our Martian might conclude that if literary studies have survived the last decade in any shape at all, it is rather owing to the practical recognition that society needs 'any discipline graduates' to staff its administrative and communicational institutions than to the social theory of the Treasury or the attitudes of leading intellectuals. Literary studies, in other words, are held in place more by the structural integration to capitalist society of their discourses and skills than by the ideologies used by either side to defend or attack their content.

Writing as someone who is deeply invested in literary studies, and still finds nothing better than the Enlightenment postulate that a rational, philosophical, reflective class increases the tendency of the State to be just (not denying the many failures), it is very hard for me to accept that what may matter most about the brilliantly radical book by a professor or essay by a student is not that it is able to liberate thought from the ossified and conventional, but that formally it corresponds to conventions that ensure the critique remains within authorised institutional structures. The professor gets good reviews, promotion, and higher ranking in the pension funds of our society. The student gets the first-class degree and the government stipend for further study. Success in this genre strengthens the idea of the intellectual as someone who is outside the system of meaning conventions, a rational professional knower who, even when becoming nominally politically engaged, respects above all the rules of the game. 'Learning' has now become such an established part of the educational state apparatus and adjunct to the culture industry that its ability to transform must seriously be in doubt.

There are not many of us (or many parts of us) that would want it otherwise. We are too much invested in our careers, and Reason, despite its fictions and falsehoods, still seems the best preventative of political tyranny. (Its integration with economic tyranny is too complex an issue for the current essay.) A detached, scholarly, rational and scientific education in the ways the world has been represented is devoutly to be wished, and at other times and places I would argue there is not enough of such learning. Nonetheless, under scrutiny, the way we direct expression of this learning to the literary essay seems at best fainthearted and at worst deeply conservative. Paraphrasing Marx, we teach students 'to understand' the text when the point is to change it. Critics may claim to change the text by showing how it is different from what it appears to be, but our teaching how to 're-read' merely keeps the resulting transform-ation of consciousness within the head of the informed and isolated knower, even when these knowers grandly configure themselves as 'interpretive communities' (for which read, sub-sub-sections of this or that theoretical tendency). As what is re-read is not re-written, but merely re-read and re-read again and again, so it becomes more and more apparent that the originating text is completely untouched by the hermeneutical process and never twice the same. The activity of academic literary criticism is losing contact with its object.

Thoughts such as these have led me to experiment with using rewriting as a form of literary training and assessment. As is evident, the rationale is multi-layered. In kernel form, it is that students should return their critical and theoretical knowledge to the originating text by re-writing it. Students should not see themselves as readers outside the processes of meaning-formation, lucidly criticising them. They should learn the disciplines and benefits of this fiction of impartiality, and then pass beyond them by putting themselves back into the work of re-creation. Ideally they thus become active re-makers of their world, rather than cleverly passive outsiders. Since the most heavily promoted subject position in the modern world is that of spectator-consumer-voyeur, to achieve this transformation is a critically vital process. It is also justifiable in pragmatic terms as among the best ways of focusing students' interest on the formal methods and philosophical significance of texts, and in terms of training their expressive skills.

How does one go about such teaching? The only general principle is that almost anything goes, hence the fertility of the method. For example:

Benjamin Franklin's *Autobiography* has been known to freeze the hearts and minds of first year students. Ask a seminar to adopt Franklin's style and use it to write a page describing the experience of a fictional student going up to university. Circulate the result, ask students to note which aspects of Franklin's style the re-writing has successfully captured. Note these on the blackboard so they can be clearly seen. The seminar thus develops a clear critical sense of what Franklin is about, and sees how easily his discourse translates into modern experience.

Re-evaluating and re-positioning first-person narrators is valuable primary work. Henry James's 'Daisy Miller' is told from a point of view which is either that of Winterbourne or that of James. Free indirect style is used to elide the difference. Ask students to clarify the difference, or to imagine a woman writer telling the story from a point of view which is intimate with Daisy in the way James is intimate with Winterbourne.

Dickens is frequently described as melodramatic. Ask a group of students to act out any scene of confrontation or emotional intensity. Try out *different* body positions and intonations. Ask the watching group of students to make notes about what is being expressed thematically in the scene, then re-enact the enactment with the shadow-group articulating what the text implies but likes to leave unsaid. This exercise usually makes concretely evident how Dickens relies on caricature as a form of repressive role-typing, and then draws enormous power from the political and sexual energies cathected by the process.

The narrative sequence of *The Great Gatsby* represents Gatsby's courtship of Daisy in retrospect. Ask students to re-order the story in historical chronological sequence. At the same time, note that Fitzgerald communicates thought through visual images and metaphors. Take a specimen page or paragraph and put the character's thoughts into more conventional free indirect style. These transformations show how Fitzgerald's novel has rewritten the basic elements of materialist love romance into a text that is at the same time the apotheosis of the desire-structure of his society, and its would-be critical representation.

As these specimen exercises indicate, it is possible to encourage students to rewrite texts in ways that require very little more skill than typical critical assignments or exercises in practical criticism. The process of doing this demystifies the text by showing it as the product of practical decisions (conscious or unconscious) about the form of communication, and as a mediator of values which can be either accepted by the reader or disputed. Above all, rewriting makes clear how texts enter our minds, how we are construed by them, and how we can transform our response by transforming them in return.

Using rewriting as a critical-creative practice makes everyone aware of the importance of rewriting in the production of our literary tradition. This awareness is in itself very beneficial because it undermines the still potent ideology that great texts are 'original' (points of origin for sense) and that great writing is simply a matter of genius. When students see literature as conventional and repetitious, they feel much more equipped to understand its systems, much more able to apprentice themselves to learning, and much more able to appreciate the skill of a writer who does brilliantly what others have done well. They can also develop a sense of the endlessly fertile cross-relations that constitute the literary field, a sense which I find especially valuable at a time when the surfeit of texts produced by the culture industry encourages students to impose sense via one or more ever-ready theories (heuristically beneficial, let me say, but also procrustean), or by boxing texts in genres or movements or periods.

This summer term, to put some of my thinking about rewriting to a more extensive test than heretofore, I taught for the first time a seminar entitled 'Rewriting', which set out to examine texts which were explicit rewrites of others. Students would be assessed on their ability to produce their own critically informed rewrites. As texts for initial consideration I offered Defoe's *Robinson Crusoe* rewritten by J.M. Coetzee as *Foe*, by Michel Tournier as *Man Friday* and by J.G. Ballard as *Concrete Island* (plus Muriel Spark's *Robinson*, Vic Sage's story in *Dividing Lines* and Jane Gadamer's *Crusoe's Daughter*). We then read fairy stories and folk tales as rewritten by Angela Carter, Robert Coover and Donald Barthelme. And then Charlotte Bronte's *Jane Eyre*, rewritten by Jean Rhys in *Wide Sargasso Sea*. Then we looked at the rewriting of the detective story and the tale of colonial jealousy by Robbe-Grillet in *The Erasers* and *Jealousy*. I had also suggested students might like to read Jorge Luis Borges, *Labyrinths*, the crime novel as handled by William Faulkner in *Sanctuary* and rewritten by James Hadley Chase as *No Orchids for Miss Blandish*, Dickens rewritten by Sue Roe, *Estella, Her Expectations*, and Kathy Acker, *Great Expectations*; 'Scheherazade' rewritten by John Barth in *Chimera*; Nathaniel Hawthorne's *The Scarlet Letter*, rewritten by George Eliot as *Silas Marner* and by Philip Roth as *Roger's Version*, and, indeed, by Kathy Acker again in *Blood and Guts in the High School*; Tom Stoppard (all his works, especially *Travesties*, *The Real Inspector Hound*, *Rosencrantz and Guildenstern are Dead*); Freud's case histories rewritten as D.M. Thomas, *The White Hotel*; Jane Austen, *Northanger Abbey*, Brautigan, *Troutfishing in America*, *The Hawkline Monster*; Pope, *Imitations of Horace*, Lowell, *Imitations*.

As you may well imagine, we did not begin to deal with the later half of this list. In practice, each student in the group (including the teacher) was charged to bring along a rewritten text of the specified kind each week. These were read out or circulated for reading and discussions evolved from there. Through intuition or happenstance a 'core' of evolving concerns appeared early on. The endless versatility of fairy stories makes them ideal material for foregrounding the work of rewriting, as does their potent condensation of social stereotypes and myth. We evolved a trajectory through Carter, Perrault, Maitland, Coover, Propp on the folk tale, Stone on fairy-tale motifs in Dickens, Bettelheim on the uses of enchantment, Freudian analysis, leading to Cinderella/Sleeping Beauty/Beauty and the Beast/Bluebeard resonances in *Jane Eyre*. An impromptu discussion of the fairy-tale references in the film *Pretty Woman* and the ancient version of the fiction, Ovid's account of Pygmalion, led on to the decision to read a Mills and Boon romance and discussions of whether or not such a popular genre, written to formula, could ever be rewritten, since it was already the prescribed rewriting of an already rewritten idea.

These discussions were some of the best seminar discussions I have had for a long time, partly because they were without the secret agenda I usually carry into the room ('Ah yes, this is Defoe, now we ought to deal with imperialism, commodity, travel writing, spiritual autobiography, the mercantile versus the gentry and the criminal underclass, expansion of publishing, democracy etc. etc.'). The students found their own levels of engagement *inside* the text and as they talked them out we would find questions probing everywhere and anywhere – sexual politics, Freudian theory, the structure of romance, what Victorian life 'was really like', as opposed to its fictional representation. The topics covered were those that would come up in any university seminar, but there was always a sense of their arising out of personal engagement with the activity of rewriting. The agenda was not academic but intellectual. This inevitably provoked occasional bouts of nerves. How did all this 'fit into' the syllabus? How did it prepare for final examinations? Was it right to be having so much fun? But there was no doubt in anyone's mind at the end of term that they had gained in confidence in relation to literature, and learnt something at a deeper level than most seminars usually reach.

Another notable feature of the seminar was the way in which we all learned from each other. Since there was no ideal target object for our writing – the first-class essay showing mastery of scholarly materials – everyone was much more interested in drawing benefit from the contributions of everyone else. One student's interest in romantic fiction led another to formulate a typical romance scenario which everyone then fleshed out in their own manner. An early playful suggestion, drawn from Tournier, that Robinson might have discovered in his island isolation homoerotic and cannibal tendencies, may have helped inform one of the example pieces which follows. The process of learning from each other fostered the highest educational achievement: it created confidence and trust in the process of working together critical reflection and imaginative play in language, for the self and with others.

APPENDIX: Four example pieces of rewriting

1

Mermaid and Prince

By Sean O'Reilly

'Take me as far up the beach as you can,' said the mermaid firmly. The wave swelled and quickened the speed of its right flank. This was the wave her father had given her on the day she was first allowed to rise alone to the surface of the water. Her sisters' waves might be swifter and more graceful, but they were also more obedient. They would never dare adventure beyond the boundaries of her father's kingdom. For her sisters that was not even a restriction. They were content to pass their three hundred years of existence gliding wishfully around their father's gardens, and wondering at the meanings of the sun's rays when they pierced deep enough into the sea to form ephemeral patterns on the sea bed.

'As far as you can,' encouraged the mermaid, lifting her tail up over her head. The wave bulged massively and propelled her across the hissing sand. She felt there was something strange about the way it withdrew from under her, caressing her back and tail sadly, and lingering on the tangled hair at the top of her neck as though it were making a secret, final goodbye. The mermaid screamed. There was no sign of it gathering again offshore. The sea was unmoved by her mermaid whistle. The wave had died.

It had served her faithfully for more than ten years. Without the wave's patient resilience she would never have managed to carry the Prince to this unknown island where she could hold him prisoner, and later it was the wave's idea to bring another man, a different sort of man with dark skin, whom the Prince was forced to befriend or kill.

The mermaid sat up on the warm sand and studied the dagger in her hand. The blade, a thin spike of silver, had been broken from the crown of the great Sea-King. The handle was a chunk of unfashioned diamond slit by a bolt of gold. This dagger might have saved the life of her youngest sister whose voice was more beautiful and clear than any other creature under the waves. Ships passing above whilst she was singing would haul in their sails and listen in silence to the mysterious music. Sometimes one of the sailors would lose control and plunge into the sea. Swimming up excitedly to meet him, the sisters would grab hold of his hands and feet and lead him down to their father's gardens.

One day it was a handsome black-eyed Prince they found floundering in the water. He said he had come to discover what had happened to the men of his crew who had leapt overboard in search of the wonderful music. They laughed and brought him to where the youngest was singing and combing her hair, but instead of their customary games of teasing and flirting until the man's last breath was gone over his head, the youngest mermaid pleaded with her sisters to let the Prince live and return to his ship.

The young mermaid had fallen in love with the black-eyed Prince, and the prospect of an eternal soul if he chose to marry her. To the sea-witch she sacrificed her beautiful voice in return for a pair of human legs, in spite of the risk of being turned to scum on the swaying face of the sea if the Prince's heart joined with another. But the Prince could only love the frail mute girl like a child, and he took someone else for his wife. The sisters hurried to the sea-witch in desperation. She demanded handfuls of their long golden hair as the price for a dagger with which the young mermaid might kill her Prince and free herself from her encroaching fate as endlessly drifting foam. The dagger tempted the young mermaid for an instant only. After kissing the foreheads of the sleeping Prince and his new bride, she waved to her sisters and slid quietly into the water. On board the wedding ship there were shouts and alarms. 'The girl without a tongue has fallen overboard,' they called.

Taking the dagger in both hands the mermaid drove it into the flesh of her left breast. A cold pain spread across her chest and shoulder. Warm blood flowed down her belly to her scaly hips where it turned blue. Another sharp pain began at the back of her eyes. She lay back on the sand savouring the disquiet she felt in her heart.

It would not be long before the Prince began his morning inspection of the beach. During the first year of his captivity she used to dream up ways to torment him. The single footprint was the shrewdest idea – the foot of a drowned corpse marking the sand in the instant before the waves retreat. It sent him mad for days. She thought he would never leave his watch by the bonfire on the hill. A few days later she left three footprints for him, an infant's and a young girl's, and a man's with the big toe missing. She studied his reactions carefully. Collapsing to his knees he vomited over himself and lay on the sand without moving. A little later he sat up suddenly and began to masturbate furiously, but before he had finished he began to cry and fled inland. The footprints were gone when he returned, carrying a sunshade made from chicken feathers proudly across his shoulder, and in their place was the naked body of a freshly drowned woman. He tried slapping her face, and pulling open her eyelids to see her pupils, and finally he turned her over to massage her lungs. In the end he saw it was useless and relented to her death, but his submission brought about a comical change. He fell on the girl's body violently, his kisses becoming bites until he was ripping the skin from her belly and breasts with his teeth. His face and beard covered with blood he forced her legs apart and pushed himself inside her. He didn't tire until dusk. Taking hold of her by the hair he dragged her back to his enclosure, leaving his sunshade casting a shadow over the stained, scattered sand.

The handle of the dagger glowed in her breast. The stone rubbed and scraped her nipple when she breathed. Blood had collected in a thickening pool around her navel. The Prince would discover her, pity, her, perhaps recognise her, and tend her until she was well, and during that time she would make sure he fell in love with her. It would not be very difficult. After all, his ten years of captivity had been shaped and planned to prepare for her own arrival. Unlike her youngest sister she would not have to lose her tongue or her fish's tail to win the love of a man, not to mention an eternal soul.

Two figures were coming cautiously towards her across the sand. The one in front, surely the Prince by the rings on his fingers, carried a huge staff braced with metal. The black-eyed Prince. She recalled the night of the storm, the guilty ecstasy of her desires transfigured into action as she takes herself up through the dark sea to the giant, crashing waves and the rain beating against her face. The ship holding him and his new bride tears cleanly in half. She carries the shrieking bride personally to the sea bottom and fastens her there to a stone. The waves have their orders, only one survivor, the Prince. The other bodies delivered to the sea-witch who sits feeding her toads and her serpents from her own toothless mouth. A new staircase for her house of bones.

The two figures circle her irritably. The black man scratches the streaks of salt on his bare body. The Prince pulls at his dark beard and spits. Her arrival seems to annoy them. The Prince walks a few steps away and sets his staff in the ground. He grunts something, but the black man shakes his head and crosses his arms emphatically. The mermaid can't understand what is happening. Neither of them appear to have any pity for the wounded body of the beautiful mermaid. Opening her mouth she releases a small groan. The Prince shouts again, and the black man bends awkwardly and rubs his hands. Aggravated, the mermaid realizes that he intends to return her to the water, and lashing out ferociously with her tail she strikes the black man on the chest knocking him backwards into the sea. Defiantly she turns her head towards the Prince, and at the same time reaches out her hand in appeal, as a sign that her weakness is worthy of the Prince alone. The black man returns to his side whispering enthusiastically. A hint of surprise rises in the Prince's eyes as he listens, and nodding his head in amused consent, he retrieves his staff from the sand. The mermaid searches his hard, rich black eyes for some clue to what he intends. His feet come to a halt a few steps from her face and for some reason when the mermaid notices that the hair on his toes has been singed by the fire, or maybe even the sun, she understands immediately that they have decided to eat her.

Near dusk a vaporous shape was kneeling beside the body of the mermaid. The head and fish's tail have been removed, leaving only a bruised torso punctured by a dagger which the shape seemed to touch with fondness. After a long while the insubstantial shape pulled the mermaid corpse down to the shore and back to the sea. Far overhead, in the realm above the clouds, the daughters of the air looked on, counting the tears dropping from their eyes.

2

The Poole woman sleeps...

By David Harold

'To be in love is to create a religion whose God is fallible.'
– Borges

The Poole woman sleeps and dreams Her bitch dreams of whelps crushed beneath rolls of maternal flesh. In Poole's gin bottle She can see the ship that brought Her here, directly to this room.

Is He awake? She mostly thinks not. His eyes, always so clear and cruel and startled in the day, are distant here in the darkness of the attic room. They see another world, one within, perhaps even another time. Sometimes She thinks She imagines Him, sitting in Her room in His plain nightshirt asleep in the protection of Her restraint. That would make sense to Her. She needs Him to come, so He comes. All is imagined. But no, if She stirred She could touch him. He is real. Why does He come? Because He must? Does He dream as He walks? Does He dream of another as He walks towards Her?

She sits in Her corner in Her shroud. Often She is cold. She has no underwear, She soils it. She has forgotten Her body. It is beyond Her now. But still She recites a litany of caresses to remind Her how it used to be. He is so cold to Her now. Her dreaming husband, but in His eyes She sees the permanent occluded ghost of a flame.

Sometimes they perform a trade. He is the prisoner in Her cell, imprisoned in His spent desire while She roams free in the manor. She leaves the keys to Her cell hanging loose in the lock. She looks at Jane's paintings; ice cold, evil elements; a green-tinged arm that unsettles Her; pale, ephemeral women; snow masses, the pigment of powdered bone.

Sometime before each dawn He must leave Her. If She has pleased Him He may even stay until the first dawn rays of attic day bring a hint of wakefulness to His eyes. More often She is left to contemplate the solemn dawn alone, crying out to the sun silently. The sun is so cold in this part of the world. As He rises She scampers after Him, brushes out a crease in His nightshirt, a trace of dust that would only confuse them in the morning. He is no detective. He ignores even the obvious. The metaphysical, the inexplicable is so frightening to Him. And oh, how He craves it.

She touches the girl's Puritan dresses, starched linens, barbed wool. She could not bear their restrictions on Her. She takes Her hand away feeling them smothering Her.

In the attic Her knife sits on the cold floor. Her wrists burn with Her wise insanity, in strips where He ties Her during the day.

Her skin. How it contrasts with His. When they tumbled together they were yin and yang, a single serpent endlessly devouring its own tail. Oh God! But was their passion sweet! Her skin is touched, now and forever, with His white. It stands in pale ridges where She has scarred Herself. And He, He is touched by Her dark passions. Somewhere inside.

Magic is the power of want. Is that why He walks like the zombie in the night? Magic is the power of desire. Does She desire this destruction? Is that Her madness, the curse She has inflicted on Herself, inflicted on the effigy of the red woman that she tried to become for Him? Magic is the power of imagination. She is a magnet, drawing in the future, inevitable and all-consuming.

Jane's face ... no, She cannot bear it. How many years different from Jane is She? As many as She is from Edward? Could Her hands splinter the bone in Jane's cheeks? Could Her teeth take off Jane's lips? Could She put out Jane's eyes? Or must She put out His?

She is called Jane. "Oh Jane, you are snow and I am blood – together what will we make of Him?"

The curtain in the temple She will rend in two. She will not be the bridesmaid to this sin. This sin against Her. He will leave Her protection for the final time, and She will hold the flame She has taken from His eyes.

3

Romance Scenario:

The labyrinth of Love

Blanche thought life had passed her by. Almost 33 and quite unable to find the dashing knight she so needed. She was resigned to sewing heraldic designs and tending her rose garden, that was until the mysterious stranger arrived in the quiet village of Kinneret determined to reopen the derelict stately home and its garden maze – *The Labyrinth of Love*.

He asked her to replant the roses that gave the maze its name and she became lost in his eyes.

Notes:

The hero of romance is a self-assured and wealthy male.
He reacts antagonistically to an attractive female whose allure upsets his ordered world.
She responds ambiguously, misinterpreting the hero's behaviour as less interested than it is.
Her identity is fractured and remade by her yielding to his power, a process which enables the recognition of her own passional nature.
In *The Labyrinth of Love* Adam Alexander is a capitalist emperor whose habit is cutting Gordian knots: he breaks up companies and 'liberates' their stifled energies, making lots of money in the process. Could it be that his middle name is Hanson? He is well-known for his expensive bachelor life-style. Blanche is locked in an infertile marriage with ????? and devoting her energies to charity-work.

4

Exposure

After William Owen

Over the line, I shudder in the box as the words knife us.
Wearied, we talk because the night is silent;
Low words, all old; our memories are of the salient.
Our words whisper, we are worried; silent, we are nervous ...
We are strung on the wire.

Later, and alone, we probe at the words that knife us.
Bloodied, we turn and twist them as the night is silent.
In our low words our distance and fear is what is salient;
Frightened, across the silence, we are curious, nervous ...
But we are still together.

Nothing is quite over, save the undone years;
My words in the night engage and parry yours,
We are still together, but never where we were;
Tied now in fright, in nervous fear, in war ...
Where we hang nightly, strung on the wire.

James Anderson

Bibliography

ADAMS, Richard 1980. *The Girl in a Swing*, Harmondsworth: Penguin Books.

ALTICK, R.D. 1947. 'Symphonic Imagery in *Richard II*', *PMLA*, Vol. lxii; repr. in: Nicholas Brooke (ed.), *Shakespeare: Richard II*, London: Macmillan (Casebook Series, 1973).

AUERBACH, Nina 1982. *Woman and the Demon: The Life of a Victorian Myth*, Cambridge, Ms.: Harvard University Press.

AUSTIN, J.L. 1962. *How To Do Things With Words*, Oxford: Clarendon Press.

BAKHTIN, M.M. 1981. *The Dialogic Imagination: Four Essays*, Austin: University of Texas Press.

BENJAMIN, Walter 1973. *Illuminations*, Glasgow: Fontana.

BERGONZI, Bernard 1990. *Exploding English: Criticism, Theory, Culture*, Oxford: Clarendon Press.

BHASKAR, Roy 1979. *The Possibility of Naturalism: A Philosophical Critique of the Contemporary Sciences*, Brighton: Harvester.

BRENNAN, Teresa (ed.) 1989. *Between Feminism and Psychoanalysis*, London: Routledge.

BROOKS, Cleanth 1962. 'Irony as a Principle of Structure', in: M.D. Zabel (ed.), *Literary Opinion in America*, Vol. 2, New York: Harper & Row.

BUTTER, P.H. 1962. *Edwin Muir: Man and Poet*, Edinburgh and London: Oliver & Boyd.

CHODOROW, Nancy 1978. *The Reproduction of Mothering*, Berkeley: University of California Press.

CIXOUS, Hélène 1985. *The Newly Born Woman*, Minneapolis: University of Minnesota Press.

CONRAD, Joseph 1985. *Heart of Darkness*, Harmondsworth: Penguin Books.

CORNILLON, Susan K. (ed.) 1972. *Images of Women in Fiction: Feminist Perspectives*, Bowling Green, Ohio: Bowling Green Popular Press.

CULLER, Jonathan 1975. *Structuralist Poetics: Structuralism, Linguistics and the Study of Literature*, London: Routledge & Kegan Paul.

CULLEY, Margo, and PORTUGES, Catherine 1985. *Gendered Subjects: The Dynamics of Feminist Teaching*, Boston: Routledge.

DE BEAUVOIR, Simone 1953. *The Second Sex*, Harmondsworth: Penguin Books.

DE LA MARE, Walter 1942. 'Seaton's Aunt', in: *Best Short Stories of Walter de la Mare*, London: Faber and Faber.

DE MAN, Paul 1971. *Blindness and Insight: Essays in the Rhetoric of Contemporary Criticism*, New York: Oxford University Press.

DE MAN, Paul 1984. *The Rhetoric of Romanticism*, New York and London: Columbia University Press.

DIJKSTRA, Bram 1986. *Idols of Perversity: Fantasies of Feminine Evil in Fin-de-Siècle Culture*, London: Oxford University Press.

DODSWORTH, Martin (ed.) 1989. *English Economiz'd: English and British Higher Education in the Eighties*, London: John Murray.

DONNER, H.W. 1951. *Svenska Översättningar av Shakespeares Macbeth*, Acta Academiae Aboensis, Humaniora XX/1.

DONOVAN, Josephine (ed.) 1975. *Feminist Literary Criticism*, Lexington: University Press of Kentucky.

DONOVAN, Josephine 1985. *Feminist Theory: The Intellectual Traditions of American Feminism*, New York: Frederick Ungar.

EAGLETON, Terry 1975. *Myths of Power: A Marxist Study of the Brontës*, London: Macmillan.

EAGLETON, Terry 1983. *Literary Theory: An Introduction*, Oxford: Basil Blackwell.

EATON, Trevor 1966. *The Semantics of Literature*, The Hague: Mouton & Co.

ECO, Umberto 1990. 'Semiotics of Theatrical Performance', in: Dennis Walder (ed.), *Literature in the Modern World*, Oxford: Oxford University Press.

EDWARDS, Philip 1987. *Shakespeare: A Writer's Progress*, Oxford and New York: Oxford University Press.

EINERSEN, Dorrit, and NIXON, Ingeborg 1987. 'Woman as Monster: Virago and Lamia', *Angles*, 2, University of Copenhagen, pp. 3-29.

EINERSEN, Dorrit, and NIXON, Ingeborg 1989. 'Woman as Monster: Duality and Ambiguity in the Female Image', *Proceedings from the Fourth Nordic Conference for English Studies*, University of Copenhagen, pp. 615-25.

ELIOT, T.S. 1963. *Collected Poems, 1909-1962*, London: Faber and Faber.

ELLIS, Frank H. 1951. 'Gray's *Elegy*: The Biographical Problem in Literary Criticism', *PMLA*, LXVI, pp. 971-1008.

ESSLIN, Martin 1990. 'The Signs of Drama', in: Dennis Walder (ed.), *Literature in the Modern World*, Oxford: Oxford University Press.

FIGES, Eva 1970. *Patriarchal Attitudes*, London: Virago.

FIRTH, J.R. 1957. *Papers in Linguistics, 1934-1951*, London: Oxford University Press.

FISH, Stanley 1980. *Is There a Text in This Class? The Authority of Interpretive Communities*, Cambridge, Ms.: Harvard University Press.

FLAUBERT, Gustave 1903. *Correspondance*, troisième série (1854-1869), Paris: Bibliothèque-Charpentier.

FRYE, Northrop 1957. *Anatomy of Criticism*, Princeton, N.J.: Princeton University Press.

GALLOP, Jane 1982. *Feminism and Psychonalysis: The Daughter's Seduction*, London: Macmillan.

GALLOP, Jane 1985. *Reading Lacan*, Ithaca: Cornell University Press.

GARDNER, Helen 1959. *The Business of Criticism*, London: Oxford University Press.

GILBERT, Sandra M., and GUBAR, Susan 1987. *No Man's Land: The Place of the Woman Writer in the Twentieth Century*, Vol. 1: *The War of the Words*, New Haven: Yale University Press.

GILLIGAN, Carol 1982. *In a Different Voice*, Cambridge, Ms.: Harvard University Press.

GREENBLATT, Stephen 1980. *Renaissance Self-Questioning: From More to Shakespeare*, Chicago: University of Chicago Press.

GREENE, Gayle, and KAHN, Coppelia (eds) 1985. *Making a Difference: Feminist Literary Criticism*, London: Methuen.

GREER, Germaine 1986. *Shakespeare*, Oxford and New York: Oxford University Press.

HALLIDAY, M.A.K. 1973. *Explorations in the Functions of Language*, London: Edward Arnold.

HALLIDAY, M.A.K. 1975. *Learning How To Mean*, London: Edward Arnold.

HENKE, Suzette A. 1990. *James Joyce and the Politics of Desire*, New York: Routledge.

HILL, Susan 1983. *The Woman in Black*, Harmondsworth: Penguin Books.

HIRSCH, E.D. 1967. *Validity in Interpretation*, New Haven: Yale University Press.

HIRSCH, E.D. 1976. *The Aims of Interpretation*, Chicago: Chicago University Press.

HIRSCH. E.D. 1987. 'The Politics of Theories of Interpretation', in: Rick Rylance (ed.), *Debating Texts: A Reader in Twentieth-Century Literary Theory and Method*, Milton Keynes: Open University Press.

HOBSBAWM, E.J. 1987. *The Age of Empire*, London: Cardinal.

HORNEY, Karen 1967. *Feminine Psychology*, New York: Norton.

HOWARD, Elizabeth Jane 1975. 'Three Miles Up', in: *Mr Wrong*, Harmondsworth: Penguin Books.

HUME, Robert D. 1976. *The Development of English Drama in the Late Seventeenth Century*, Oxford: Clarendon Press.

HUMM, Maggie 1986. *Feminist Criticism: Women as Contemporary Critics*, Brighton, Sussex: Harvester.

HUNTLEY: J.F. 1977. 'An Objective Test for Literary Comprehension', *College English*, 39, No. 3, pp. 361-67.

IRIGARAY, Luce 1985. *This Sex Which Is Not One*, Ithaca: Cornell University Press.

JAUSS, Hans Robert 1982. *Toward an Aesthetic of Reception*, Brighton: Harvester.

JAMESON, Fredric 1983. *The Political Unconscious*, London: Methuen.

KOZICKI, Henry 1977. 'Meaning in Tennyson's *In Memoriam*', *Studies in English Literature 1500-1900*, 17, No. 4.

LAKATOS, Imre 1972. 'Falsification and the Methodology of Scientific Research Programmes', in: Imre Lakatos and Alan Musgrave (eds), *Criticism and the Growth of Knowledge*, London: Cambridge University Press.

LANGBAUM, Robert 1957. *The Poetry of Experience: The Dramatic Monologue in Modern Literary Tradition*, London: Chatto & Windus.

LEDERER, Wolfgang 1968. *The Fear of Women*, New York: Harcourt & Brace.

LEECH, G.N. 1983. *Principles of Pragmatics*, London: Longman.

LENIN, V.I. 1982. *Imperialism: The Highest Stage of Capitalism*, Moscow: Progress Publishers.

LENTRICCHIA, Frank 1983. *After the New Criticism*, London: Methuen.

LODGE, David 1977. *The Modes of Modern Writing: Metaphor, Metonymy, and the Typology of Modern Literature*, London: Edward Arnold.

LODGE, David (ed.) 1988. *Modern Criticism and Theory: A Reader*, London: Longman.

MACHEN, Arthur 1970. 'The White People', in: *Tales of Horror and the Supernatural*, London: John Baker.

MARKS, Elaine, and DE COURTIVRON, Isabelle (eds) 1981. *New French Feminisms*, New York: Schocken Books.

MARX, Karl 1975. *Early Writings*, Harmondsworth: Penguin Books.

MARX, Karl 1977. *Capital* III, New York: International Publishers.

MARX, Karl and ENGELS, Friedrich 1976. *The German Ideology*, Moscow: Progress Publishers.

McCONNELL-GINET, Sally, BORKER, Ruth, and FURMAN, Nelly (eds) 1980. *Women and Language in Literature and Society*, New York: Praeger.

McGANN, Jerome J. 1985. *The Beauty of Inflections: Literary Investigations in Historical Method and Theory*, Oxford: Clarendon Press.

MERMIN, Dorothy 1983. 'Heroic Sisterhood in *Goblin Market*', *Victorian Poetry*, 21, No. 2, pp. 107-118.

MICHIE, Helena 1983. 'The Battle for Sisterhood: Christina Rossetti's Strategies for Control in Her Sister Poems', *The Journal of Pre-Raphaelite Studies*, 3, No. 2, pp. 38-55.

MOI, Toril 1985. *Sexual/Textual Politics: Feminist Literary Theory*, London: Methuen.

MOI, Toril 1986. *The Kristeva Reader*, New York: Columbia University Press.

MOTION, Andrew 1984. *Dangerous Play: Poems 1974-1984*, Edinburgh: Salamander Press.

MULLINS, Edwin 1985. *The Painted Witch*, London: Secker and Warburg.

MULRYNE, J.R. 1965. *Shakespeare: Much Ado About Nothing*, London: Edward Arnold (Studies in English Literature, No. 16).

NEWTON, Judith, and ROSENFELT, Deborah (eds) 1985. *Feminist Criticism and Social Change*, New York: Methuen.

NICHOLSON, Linda (ed.) 1990. *Feminism/Postmodernism*, New York: Routledge.

OATES, J.C. 1991. 'A Novelist Finds the Bare Bones of a Play', *Modern Drama*, 34, No. 1.

OHMANN, Richard 1971. 'Speech Acts and the Definition of Literature', *Philosophy and Rhetoric*, 4, pp. 1-19.

PETERSEN, Per S. 1980. 'Litteraturvidenskaben i engelskstudiet: dadaisme eller rationalisme', in: Hans Hauge og Per S. Petersen (eds), *Tekstvidenskaben i engelskstudiet: bidrag til en principdebat*, The Dolphin, 3, University of Aarhus.

PETERSEN, Per S. forthcoming. 'Literary Studies between Theoreticism and Pragmatism: Curricular Designing in the English Departments of the Danish Universities of Aarhus, Copenhagen, and Odense', in Inger Kabell and Jørgen Erik Nielsen (eds), *English in Denmark*, POET, 18, University of Copenhagen.

POPPER, Karl R. 1972. *Objective Knowledge: An Evolutionary Approach*, Oxford: Clarendon Press.

SAID, Edward 1983. *The World, the Text, and the Critic*, London: Faber & Faber.

SANSOM, William 1956. 'A Woman Seldom Found', in: *A Contest of Ladies*, London: Hogarth Press.

SCHMIDT, S.J. 1982. *Foundation for the Empirical Study of Literature: The Components of a Basic Theory*, Hamburg: Helmut Buske.

SCHOLES, Robert 1985. *Textual Power: Literary Theory and the Teaching of English*, New Haven and London: Yale University Press.

SEBEOK, Thomas A. (ed.) 1960. *Style in Language*, Cambridge, Ms.: MIT Press.

SELDEN, Raman 1989. *Practising Theory and Reading Literature: An Introduction*, Hemel Hempstead: Harvester Wheatsheaf.

SELL, Roger D. 1989. 'English Departments in British Higher Education: A View from Abroad', in: Dodsworth 1989:89-100.

SELL, Roger D. (ed.) 1991. *Literary Pragmatics*, London: Routledge.

SELL, Roger D. forthcoming (a). 'Literary Pragmatics', *The Encyclopedia of Language and Linguistics*, Pergamon Press and Aberdeen University Press.

SELL, Roger D. forthcoming (b). 'Literary Gossip, Literary Theory, and Literary Pragmatics', in: Roger D. Sell and Peter Verdonk (eds), *Poetics, Linguistics, Society*.

SHOWALTER, Elaine (ed.) 1985. *The New Feminist Criticism: Essays on Women, Literature and Theory*, New York: Pantheon Books.

SINFIELD, Alan 1985. 'Introduction to Part II: Reproductions, Interventions', in: Jonathan Dollimore and Alan Sinfield (eds), *Political Shakespeare*, Manchester: Manchester University Press.

TAYLOR, Gary 1983. 'The Date and Authorship of the Folio Version', in: Gary Taylor and Michael Irwin (eds), *The Division of the Kingdoms: Shakespeare's Two Versions of King Lear*, Oxford: Clarendon Press ('reprinted new as paperback', 1986).

VERSCHUEREN, J. 1987. *Pragmatics as a Theory of Linguistic Adaptation*, IRPA [International Pragmatics Association], Working Document 1.

WAUGH, Patricia 1989. *Feminine Fictions: Revisiting the Postmodern*, London: Routledge.

WARNER, Sylvia Townsend 1978. *Lolly Willowes*, London: Women's Press.

WEEDON, Chris 1987. *Feminist Practice and Poststructuralist Theory*, Oxford: Basil Blackwell.

WELDON, Fay 1980. *Puffball*, London: Hodder and Stoughton.

WELDON, Fay 1983. *The Life & Loves of a She-Devil*, London: Hodder and Stoughton.

WELLEK, René, and WARREN, Austin 1956. *Theory of Literature*, New York: Harcourt, Brace & World, Inc.

WILLIAMS, Raymond 1977. *Marxism and Literature*, Oxford: Oxford University Press.

WILLIAMS, Raymond 1983. *Writing in Society*, London: Verso.